THE HOOFP

M000304442

The Wild Horses
of Ocracoke

THE HOOFPRINTS GUIDE TO

The Wild Horses
of Ocracoke

Written and Illustrated by
Bonnie U. Gruenberg

The Hoofprints Guide to the Wild Horses of Ocracoke

Copyright © 2015 by Bonnie U. Gruenberg.

ISBN 13: 978-1-941700-15-0

Library of Congress Control Number: 2015952626

Published by Quagga Press, an imprint of Synclitic Media, LLC
1646 White Oak Road • Strasburg, PA 17579 • www.quaggapress.com

Also by the author
> *The Wild Horse Dilemma: Conflicts and Controversies of the Atlantic Coast Herds* (Quagga Press, 2015)
> *The Hoofprints Guide Series* (Quagga Press, 2015)
> > Assateague • Chincoteague • Corolla
> > Ocracoke • Shackleford Banks • Cumberland Island
> *Essentials of Prehospital Maternity Care* (Prentice Hall, 2005)
> *Birth Emergency Skills Training: Manual for Out-of-hospital Providers* (Birth Guru/Birth Muse, 2008)
> *Hoofprints in the Sand Wild Horses of the Atlantic Coast* (as Bonnie S. Urquhart; Eclipse Press, 2002)
> *The Midwife's Journal* (Birth Guru/Birth Muse, 2009)
> *Hoofprints in the Sand: Wild Horses of the Atlantic Coast*, Kindle Edition (Quagga Press, 2014)
> *Wild Horses of the Atlantic Coast: An Intimate Portrait*, Kindle Edition (Quagga Press, 2014)

Forthcoming
> *Wild Horse Vacations: Your Guide to the Atlantic Wild Horse Trail with Local Attractions and Amenities*(Quagga Press, 2015)
> > Vol. 1: Assateague, MD | Chincoteague, VA | Corolla, NC
> > Vol. 2: Ocracoke, NC | Shackleford Banks, NC | Cumberland Island, GA
> *Wild Horses! A Kids' Guide to the East Coast Herds* (Quagga Press, 2015)
> *Birth Emergency Skills Training*, 2nd Edition (Synclitic Press, 2015).

Ocracoke Island was home to the world's only mounted Boy Scout troop. Photograph courtesy of the Ocracoke Preservation Society.

Introduction

"But they aren't wild!" my son said, disappointed. He rattled a stick between the slats of the pen to get the ponies' attention while his brother balanced near the top hoping to spot a wild herd from his vantage point. All they saw were several decidedly domestic-looking specimens dismantling a pile of hay. We had visited parts of Cape Hatteras National Seashore several times beginning in the early 1990s, but this was our first visit to Ocracoke. We had ventured this far in search of Banker horses, which we expected to find roaming freely.

Bryan stopped banging the stick when he paused to read the National Park Service signboard. "It says here that Ocracoke hasn't had wild ponies since the 1950s. The ones in the corrals are all that's left of the wild herd."

"Wow, it's like they are living history," said Keith, looking at the small group with renewed interest. "Their great-grandparents—and the great-grandparents of their great-grandparents—ran wild here for hundreds of years!" We had come to find wild ponies, but evidently had arrived some 40-odd years too late.

We didn't realize that the back story would be even more interesting than finding a free-roaming herd in residence on this shifting ribbon of sand. As it turned out, the history of the wild horses of Ocracoke wove itself around surprising subjects as dissimilar as colonial farmers and fishermen, Spanish explorers, Boy Scouts, shipwrecks, geography, and pirates.

When I first started researching the wild horses in the mid-1990s, I was surprised to find that wild horses lived on a number of Atlantic barrier islands and had once ranged along much of the Atlantic coast. They made their first hoofprints there not long after the arrival of early European settlers, and in time they ran free on innumerable North American islands and peninsulas from the Caribbean to Canada. I learned that small herds remained on the coast of Virginia, North Carolina, Maryland, and Georgia; on Sable Island, off Nova Scotia, Canada; and on Great Abaco Island in the Bahamas. Each population of horses has its own character, its own history, and its own set of problems. In most cases, these animals have made a unique contribution to local history, and each herd has its own detractors and defenders.

After my first book, *Hoofprints in the Sand: Wild Horses of the Atlantic Coast*, was published in 2002 by Eclipse Press, I dove in deeper, interviewing experts, evaluating the evidence, and monitoring the herds. I explored management conflicts that encompassed political, economic, and cultural issues as well as purely scientific ones. I studied storms and shipwrecks, equine behavior and genetics, history, epidemiology, barrier-island dynamics, sea-level rise, beach development, and the perpetual clash of viewpoints. I studied hundreds of documents, from historical papers to scholarly journals to court transcripts, so that I might accurately present the pertinent issues. Distilling all this information, I tried to present all sides of the issues fairly so that readers might reach their own conclusions. The result is *The Wild Horse Dilemma: Conflicts and Controversies of the Atlantic Coast Herds* (Quagga Press, 2015) the most comprehensive work ever published about these horses.

Wild Horse Dilemma is exhaustively researched, copiously documented, and peer-reviewed; but at 600 pages it may be too long for many people eager to learn about a particular herd. For readers with limited time, I created the Hoofprints Series. Excerpted from *Wild Horse Dilemma* and containing additional photographs, each Hoofprints book presents a single Atlantic Coast herd in sufficient detail to satisfy both the layman and the academic.

I take all my wild-horse photographs though telephoto lenses that let me to keep my distance. When horses approach, I retreat. My goal has been to remain so peripheral to their lives, they will forget that I am nearby. Because countless people have stroked them, fed them, and lured them, some can be momentarily docile, occasionally indifferent, or routinely bold and pushy in the presence of people. As anyone bitten or trampled can attest, they are no less wild than horses that avoid human contact. When we impose ourselves and our desires on their lives, when we habituate them to our presence, when we teach them to approach us for food and attention, we rob them of their wildness. When we treat them as we would their domestic counterparts, we miss the opportunity to observe them in a natural state, that is, to appreciate the things that make them irresistibly attractive.

We miss the very point of driving past thousands of their tame kin to seek them out. We create something like a petting zoo hazardous to us and to them. If we truly love and respect wild creatures, we must learn to stand back and enjoy watching them from afar. Only then can they—and we—know the real meaning of wildness.

As the earth's dominant species, we have the power to preserve or destroy the wildlife of the world and the ecosystems in which they live. The choices we make regarding wild horses are far-reaching. We alter their destiny whether we act or choose to do nothing. We can begin to deal wisely with wild horses by understanding the facts and discovering how the threads of their existence are woven into the tapestry of life. Only through understanding can we hope to make rational, educated decisions about the welfare of these fascinating, inspiring animals.

Bonnie U. Gruenberg
Strasburg, Pennsylvania
September 1, 2015

Photograph by Aycock Brown, courtesy of the Outer Banks History Center.

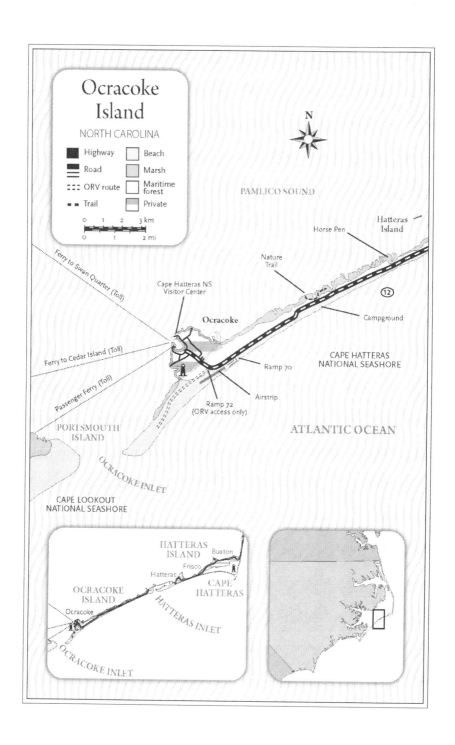

On March 22, 2010, a celebrity came to Ocracoke Island. She arrived secretly in the dark of night, and on discovering her, the paparazzi plastered her photographs all over the Internet. The starlet was oblivious to the fanfare, being a newborn filly with nothing on her mind but frolic and sunshine.

Paloma, as she was later named, captivated the audience by capering around her patient dam, Spirit. Her base coat was bay, accented with four high, white stockings and a large diamond on her forehead. Like her dam, she displayed a white pinto marking, looking for all the world as if some troublemaker had upended a paint bucket over her back.

Paloma's instant celebrity went well beyond the public's fascination with whiskery new foals. Before 2009, the Ocracoke herd mostly comprised elderly horses and those unsuitable for breeding. It appeared that this historic herd was spiraling toward inevitable extinction. Under the advice of Dr. Sue Stuska of Cape Lookout National Seashore, two stallions and two mares from Shackleford Banks had arrived to invigorate the genome with new bloodlines from a very old breed. When Spirit became romantically involved with Wenzel, a diminutive bay Shackleford stud, the result was Paloma.

Ocracoke Island lies east-southeast of the mouth of the Pamlico River, about 30 mi/38 km from the nearest point on the mainland. A pearl in the barrier island necklace, Ocracoke is separated from Hatteras Island by Hatteras Inlet to the northeast, and from Portsmouth Island by Ocracoke Inlet to the southwest. An earlier Hatteras Inlet, which closed around 1755, once crossed the barrier chain about 7.5 mi/12.2 km farther east, just beyond Quork Hammock, across the lower end of the present Tar Hole Beach. When Old Hatteras Inlet was open, what is now the northeastern part of Ocracoke was part of Hatteras Island. When the inlet closed, *all* of Ocracoke became part of Hatteras Island. Ocracoke did not regain its independence until September 7, 1846, when New Hatteras Inlet opened in the same storm that created Oregon Inlet.

Ocracoke remains an appealing Outer Banks outpost, all the more endearing for its inaccessibility. Because it is still a village of working watermen, it has escaped some of the artificiality of other resort communities. Most visitors arrive by one of three ferry routes—the one from Hatteras is free. The Park Service manages most of this island, and as a result it remains devoid of homes and businesses along the entire 12-mi/19-km drive from the ferry dock to the village.

As elsewhere on the Banks, Highway 12 has been repeatedly relocated in response to beach recession, and it remains in jeopardy. The artificial dune ridges are unstable and are affected by overwash in every severe storm, in spite of the fact that free-roaming livestock were removed more than 50 years ago.

Barrier islands are always new, constantly shifted and rearranged by the elements, yet a feeling of timelessness awaits the visitor who hikes beyond the developed areas of Ocracoke. Parts of the island probably look about the same as they did centuries ago, when there were hundreds of free-roaming horses and cattle over the next dune. This timelessness is one of the reasons people keep coming back to Ocracoke. Schedules and deadlines are less important here, and many who spend time on the island gradually subside into the ageless rhythm of tides, moons, and seasons.

Horses once ran free on Ocracoke, but their liberty came to an abrupt halt soon after the island was designated a national seashore. Paloma and her family reside in the Ocracoke Pony Pen, a handicapped-accessible facility that allows visitors a chance to get a close look at the horses. In all seasons, the Pony Pen is a popular attraction for thousands of visitors. A brief synopsis of their supposed origins stands mounted on a plaque in front of the paddock.

As with all Banker Horses, legends, theories, and a few definite facts vie to explain their history. Misinformation appears in print so often that it passes for fact. Much is open to speculation. To understand how Spanish-blooded herds came to run wild on such unlikely outposts as North Carolina barrier islands, one must consider how and when Europeans brought horses to the North American continent, how these animals were used and maintained, and the trends and events that gave rise to unique American breeds.

The first horses reintroduced to the New World came with Columbus's second expedition in December 1493, when 1–3 dozen were

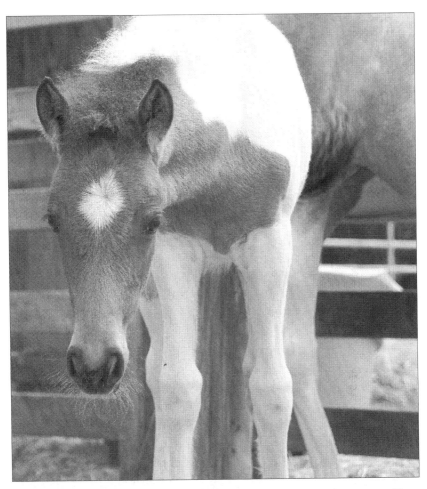

Paloma, born in 2010, holds the promise of the future in her genes. Her pinto coloration, however, as well as her dam's graying coat result from introductions of outside horses within the past five or six decades.

unloaded in Hispaniola. For the following 30 years, almost every fleet sailing from Spain to New Spain carried horses, and Hispaniola became a major equine breeding hot spot. Only about half the horses survived the 2–3-month trans-Atlantic voyages. Once the advantages of following the Atlantic currents were better understood, later colonists would typically sail from England to the West Indies before heading north to the colonies, giving them the opportunity to trade for livestock that was much more likely to survive the shorter voyage.

Thornton Chard (1940) describes many instances of early Spanish explorers bringing horses from Hispaniola to Florida, but makes a good case that none of these animals remained to reproduce; some died, some were eaten, and, some returned to the starting point. Numerous early Spanish explorers brought horses from the West Indies to what is now the United States, it does not appear that any horses started herds..

The first Spanish horses in what is now the United States were landed in Florida by Juan Ponce de Léon, who arrived in 1521 with 2 ships, 200 men, and 50 horses from Puerto Rico. They were beaten back by Calusa warriors, and de Léon was struck by a poisoned arrow. Horses were valuable at the time—Chard wrote that a single horse typically cost an astonishing 3,000–4,000 pesos (worth $18,680–24,684 in his era). His estimate is probably very low. Taking inflation into account, each horse might be worth roughly $500,000–$600,000 today, a major investment comparable with a good racehorse. Survivors would have reclaimed any serviceable horses when they withdrew to Cuba, where de Léon died of his wound.

One popular hypothesis holds that the horses on Ocracoke and elsewhere descend from stock imported for the Spanish settlement established by Lucas Vázquez de Ayllón. The evidence is sketchy at best, and virtually all credible sources disagree with one another on prominent details.

In 1521, Ayllón, a lawyer and senator in Hispaniola, aspired to discover a new territory and establish a prosperous colony there. He acquired the necessary license and dispatched Francisco Gordillo to sail north through the Bahamas to reach continental North America, instructing him to cultivate good will with the natives. (Other accounts say that Ayllón sent the ships to search for slaves.) He expected to find a legendary Indian land called Chicora, inhabited by gigantic fair-skinned natives with long, blonde hair that reached their heels.

On his journey Gordillo encountered a kinsman, Pedro de Quejo, who was on a mission to capture Indians to sell into slavery. (Or Ayllón hired Quejo to capture slaves.) Gordillo and Quejo traveled north for 8 or 9 days until they reached the mouth of a very large river, which they named for John the Baptist, *San Juan Bautista*. They believed that they found this river in latitude 33° 30'. Many modern scholars suppose that it was Winyah Bay, in the vicinity of present-day Myrtle Beach, South Carolina, if the reported latitude is accurate (it probably is not). They landed 20 men on shore and presented the Indians with gifts—then captured 70 natives and sailed away without further exploring the coast. (Or the intended purpose of their venture was to secure slaves for Ayllón.)

Ayllón was granted license to explore and occupy this territory. Legal disputes and other setbacks delayed his expedition, but in June 1526 he set sail with three large ships (or four or six), carrying "six hundred persons of both sexes" (Winsor, 1886, p. 240) (or 300), including clergymen, physicians, black slaves, goats, hogs, chickens, and 100 (or 90 or 80) Spanish horses.

They reached the mainland not at the mouth of San Juan Bautista, but at another river flowing directly into the ocean, which they believed to be at 33° 40' N. Both Winyah Bay and the Cape Fear River in North Carolina fit this description; but the actual location is widely disputed, and various sources place it anywhere from the Chesapeake region to Georgia. Soon after, Ayllón's flagship ran aground in the entrance to the river and was destroyed.

Ayllón named his discovery the River Jordan. He explored upriver but did not find a suitable settlement site, so he headed down the coast 40–50 leagues. (Because the length of a league varied, that estimate could have been anywhere from 40 to 150 mi/64–241 km.) Other sources report that he instead traveled north to follow Chesapeake Bay into Virginia and built his colony on the same site where the English would later build Jamestown.

Someplace south (or north) of his original destination, Ayllón founded the settlement of San Miguel de Gualdape in a marshy area on the River Canaan. The natives refused to feed them, then turned hostile. The starving colonists fell sick, and the slaves rebelled. The weather turned brutally cold, and the survivors fled. Ayllón died of exposure and disease in October 1526. About 150 colonists made it back to Hispaniola.

Some suggest that horses were left behind on North Carolina barrier islands after being released there to graze, safe from Indian predation. Their presence would be like living graffiti advertising Spain's claim to the land. It is more likely that any horses not eaten by the starving colonists returned with them. At the time, horses were scarce and valued highly in the New World, and every effort would have been made to keep them. Further, Ayllón's colonization attempts involved the mainland, not barrier islands, and horses left anywhere would have been fair game for the native population.

But even if this expedition did, improbably, leave horses on islands, the mouth of the Cape Fear River is about 150 mi/241 km from Ocracoke. If his colony was established at the mouth of the Pamlico or Neuse River, Ocracoke would have been closer, but records indicate that Ayllón's colony was located by a river or estuary that emptied directly into the ocean or a major arm of the ocean. The Pamlico and Neuse do not fit this description.

Historically, free-roaming horses have grazed on many of the islands of the east coast. While opening and closing of inlets might eventually allow horses placed anywhere on a barrier chain to migrate elsewhere on that chain, horses could not have traveled from Cape Fear to Ocracoke without the assistance of people.

Rather than leaving stock on barrier islands, Ayllón's sick, starving colonists probably would have slaughtered any remaining horses for sustenance. Other settlers were certainly not above eating their horses. In 1527, Narvaez landed 600 colonists at Tampa Bay, Florida; every last horse was eventually slaughtered to sustain the starving people. In Jamestown, Virginia, after all the cattle, hogs, and horses had been consumed, a few planters ate an Indian (or several) during the Starving Time. One man even ate his own wife, according to John Smith (1624) and others.

Other early explorers imported horses to the North American continent. In 1538, Hernando De Soto sailed from Spain to Santiago, Cuba, with nine vessels and 600 men, then brought a contingent of horses to his encampment on Tampa Bay. On August 1, 1539, he set out to explore what is now Florida, Alabama, and Mississippi with 500 men and 200 horses, most of them probably purchased in Cuba. Most were killed in battles with indigenous people. Chard writes, "As all seem to be accounted for it is safe to say that they left no progeny east of the Mississippi" (1940, p. 93). In 1558 a Spanish expedition from Mexico attempted to colonize present-day Parris Island, South Carolina. Of the 240 horses loaded onto the ships at the outset of the voyage, only 130 survived. Ultimately, there was insufficient food to sustain the colony, and both horses and humans became weak and emaciated. Here again, the colonists survived by eating their cattle, hogs, and horses.

Similarly, Pedro Menéndez de Aviles established permanent settlements in St. Augustine and San Mateo in Florida, which included many horses; but by 1572, colonists were starving and had eaten them. St. Augustine was resupplied with horses as the colony rallied. The Timucua and other tribes probably acquired their horses from colonists of St. Augustine, and these horses apparently gave rise to the Seminole breed, named for an ethnic group that did not exist till the 18th century. Seminole and Chickasaw Horses remained for centuries pure lines derived from the original Jennet.

None of the English settlers who filled the vacuum that Spain left in North America mentioned finding horses or any other familiar livestock grazing in the marshes when they alighted. In the early 1950s David Quinn compiled and annotated nearly all the known English and Spanish records of the Raleigh colonies in *The Roanoke Voyages* (1955), which remains the standard work on the subject. Even in this definitive form, the 16th-century sources are incomplete and often puzzling. The surviving documents say little about livestock anywhere and almost nothing about horses in and around the Roanoke Island colony. One can only speculate about the numbers and kinds of domestic livestock introduced by the colonists and what happened to those animals during and after occupation.

Thomas Harriot was the scientific advisor for the Lane colony of 1585. His *Briefe and True Report of the New Found Land of Virginia* (1590) was the first remotely scientific treatise on North America, and it influenced European thought and exploration for two centuries. He describes native animals and plants in detail, from cacti to the now-extinct Carolina parakeet, but never mentions horses.

In 1585 Sir Richard Grenville set sail for Roanoke Island in command of a flotilla laden with colonists and some of the supplies that they needed to survive in the New World. Along the way, they acquired many tropical plants, such as pineapples, which they expected to cultivate in the warm climate of Roanoke Island, but were thwarted by the unexpectedly cold winters that the region endured during the Little Ice Age. Two decades later, John Smith mused, "The sommer is hot as in *Spaine*; the winter colde as in *Fraunce* or *England*. . . . The colde is extreame sharpe. . . . In the yeare 1607 was an extraordinary frost in most of *Europe*, and this frost was founde as extreme in *Virginia*" (1612/1910, pp. 47–48).

Stopping at Puerto Rico, Grenville built a replacement for the pinnace he had lost, reunited with one of his missing ships, and obtained the horses shown in John White's watercolor of the fortified camp. Continuing to Hispaniola for more livestock, including additional horses, Grenville captured two Spanish ships.

According to the log of Grenville's flagship, the *Tiger*, while in Hispaniola Grenville traded for "horses [stallions], mares, kyne [cattle], buls, goates, swine, sheepe . . . and such like commodities of the island" (Quinn, 1955, p. 187). Evidently any livestock that survived the voyage were not enough to adequately supply the colony. On September 3, 1585, the governor of the new colony, Ralph Lane, wrote, "if Virginia had but Horses and Kine in some reasonable proportion . . . no realme in Christendome were comparable to it" (Quinn, 1955, p. 208).

Grenville himself sailed on the *Tiger*, so he may have assigned the chore of transporting livestock to other vessels in the group. Unfortunately, his ship ran aground repeatedly at Wococon (probably Ocracoke Inlet or one of its predecessors), necessitating repairs. There is some indication that plants and seeds that the colonists intended to grow in Virginia were damaged or destroyed aboard the *Tiger* during its eventful passage through the inlet. Some writers suggest that livestock were thrown overboard to lighten the foundered ship; the animals then swam to the island and escaped to run wild on Ocracoke. Documents do not mention livestock on the *Tiger* or any other vessel, however, and there is no evidence to support (or undermine) this supposition.

Like the rest of the Outer Banks, Ocracoke was long used for grazing livestock. Because horses and cattle roamed rest of the Outer Banks from 1660s to the 1930s, it is likely that livestock was also established on Ocracoke long before records reflect their introduction. At various times, Cape Hatteras and Ocracoke were connected by land, and herds on the two islands probably mingled.

Local herdsmen grazed sheep, cattle, pigs, goats, and horses free-range in the marshes, fencing their homesites against the depredations of hungry livestock. They bought, sold, and bred horses, transported them by land and water, and let them roam and mix at will. Sometimes they added outside horses to the islands, largely by introducing animals from other islands or the local mainland.

An Accurate Map of North and South Carolina With Their Indian Frontiers, by Henry Mouzon (1775). Public domain via Wikimedia Commons.

Historically, the Ocracoke horses were genetically most similar to those at Currituck Banks, Shackleford Banks, Carrot Island, and Cedar Island. A Currituck Banker born in 1913 described cattle drives from Oregon Inlet to Wash Woods, almost 60 miles, as late as the interwar years of the 20th century. Horse penning was probably of a similar scope, and the gathering likely mixed bands, disrupted harem leadership, and redefined home ranges. The dynamic nature of barrier islands, always separating and reuniting, also shuffled the genetic deck by allowing horses to migrate and find new mates.

The Banks from Chicamacomico (now the villages of Waves, Salvo, and Rodanthe) to Ocracoke were united from 1755 to 1846, save one short-lived inlet. It was possible to walk from Hatteras to Ocracoke; in fact, one of the early Cape Hatteras light keepers commuted over land from Ocracoke to tend the light. Often, there was only one shallow inlet between Portsmouth and Shackleford. Currituck Banks had as many as three open inlets at a time before 1828. Since the early 19th century, shoreline has extended in an unbroken sandy corridor from Cape Henry at the mouth of Chesapeake Bay to Oregon or New Inlet.

Barrier islands are strong, flexible barricades that mitigate ocean waves and lessen their effect on the mainland. The islands change shape to absorb the large waves of a storm and respond to sea-level rise by migrating westward, remaining more or less intact and maintaining about the same distance from the mainland.

The beaches maintain a dynamic equilibrium with sea-level change, wave energy, the availability of sand, and the shape of the beach— when one element shifts, the others adapt to keep the balance. A powerful storm can literally cut an island in half, creating an inlet where there was solid ground the day before. Conversely, sediment can fill in old inlets to create solid ground. These banks continuously merge and separate, connect and divide.

Barrier islands, about 2,500 in all, are found on all continents except Antarctica. They are adaptive, sometimes exhibiting characteristics more befitting a life form than a land form. Dunes suddenly wake and migrate across an island, engulfing everything in their path, then return to dormancy. Inlets open and close regularly; some migrate, others remain stable.

Evidence of this constant movement is observable by any alert visitor. For example, a walk along the beach of Currituck Banks, especially after a storm, will reveal hundreds of tree stumps. These are the remains of forests, 400–1,000 years old, that once grew on the west side of the island. Overwash moved the island westward and buried the forest, as someday the forest growing to the west today will be buried if nature has its way.

Storm surge can raise the water level on the North Carolina coast by as much as 20 ft/6 m. During severe weather, dramatic changes in features can take place over days or even hours. Within the Pea Island National Wildlife Refuge, New Inlet is now an area of flat ground where a series of inlets first appeared on maps in 1738. These inlets were small and shallow and filled in quickly because the larger Roanoke Inlet provided a more convenient outlet for the northern sounds until the early 19th century. By the time Oregon Inlet opened in 1846,

A Currituck Banks mare navigates around tree stumps at the water's edge, remnants of a forest that once grew on the soundside.

New Inlet was choked with sediment. It closed in 1922, but reopened around 1932 and remained until around 1945.

Inlet/outlet systems function as self-adjusting safety valves. They are created during storms or floods when storm surge washes a corridor through the sand. Hurricane storm surge is created by the forces of low atmospheric pressure, winds and surface currents circling around the eye, and the piling up of water pushed from the deep ocean to the shallows. The mounded water carries sand and whatever else it can pick up across the island toward the mainland.

As the storm moves away, the wind reverses direction, and the water rushes back to the sea. The sounds have a total surface area of roughly 3,000 mi^2/7,770 km^2; and can also produce a powerful storm surge. This swollen, unruly tide escapes by smashing through the barrier island into the ocean, producing an inlet by finding an outlet. If the water had no outlet, the barrier islands would function as dams, holding the excess water in the sound and increasing mainland storm damage due to flooding. Between storms, sand tends to fill the inlets.

The barrier island environment was challenging for livestock and humans alike. Herds and homesteads were equally vulnerable to the wrath of storms. Violent storms drowned countless Banker

Horses, but others survived and contributed their hardy genes to their progeny. To cope with the changes in geography, island livestock migrated to whatever solid ground existed, becoming separated from their brethren whenever an inlet blocked an old route. After horse penning, animals were often sold from island to island, remixing the herds.

Since colonial times, between Cape Lookout and the Virginia line more than two dozen inlets have existed long enough to appear on printed maps, and dozens more have appeared suddenly and closed rapidly. Roanoke Inlet, which Sir Walter Raleigh's colonists may have used, closed before 1819. It was probably located in the vicinity of Whalebone Junction, the intersection of U.S. Route 158, U.S. 64, and N.C. 12 in Nags Head. Once there were numerous inlets north of Roanoke Island, but now the entire drainage of Albemarle and Currituck sounds and their tributaries must flow around the island to exit through Oregon Inlet. Only Ocracoke inlet may have remained open since European contact. As of this writing, six inlets exist north of Cape Lookout.

Oregon Inlet, the northern boundary of Hatteras Island, formed during an 1846 hurricane about 2.5 mi/4 km north of its present location. The inlet has been moving south at the rate of about 100 ft/30 m a year for more than 160 years. It destroyed the first Bodie (pronounced "body") Island lighthouse, built to the south on Pea Island (now the northern part of Hatteras Island) in 1848. Confederates destroyed its 1859 successor, also on Pea Island. The present-day Bodie Island Lighthouse was built on the north shore of the inlet, therefore *on* Bodie Island, in 1872. Bodie Island, however, had been an extension of Currituck Banks, a peninsula, since Roanoke Inlet closed. Oregon inlet continued its journey southward and left the lighthouse standing watch farther and farther away. The Inlet migrated at rates as great as 300 ft (91 m) annually, demolishing campgrounds, parking lots, and roads and finally threatening the Coast Guard station at the south end of the Herbert Bonner Bridge, completed in 1963. Under natural conditions, Oregon Inlet would continue to move south, but at the expense of infrastructure. In 1989 the North Carolina Department of Transportation built a rock jetty to prevent the inlet from migrating further. This has temporarily arrested the south bank but not the north, causing Oregon Inlet

Hurricane Isabel slammed into the Outer Banks of North Carolina, washing out Highway 12 and breaching Hatteras Island. Photograph by Mark Wolfe (2003) courtesy of the Federal Emergency Management Agency.

to narrow and clog. Dredging is necessary to keep a channel open for boats under the highest part of the bridge.

Another good illustration of island movement is the Cape Hatteras lighthouse. When the present structure was commissioned in December 1870 (replacing one built in 1803), it stood 1,500–1,600 ft/457–488 m inland. Through the last few decades, the beach moved west to meet it. Finally the lighthouse stood right on the beach. From the 1960s, preservation attempts vied with the forces of nature: workers built three groins, rebuilt them when they failed, added reinforcements of large rocks and sandbags, repeatedly nourished the beach, and planted beds of artificial seaweed. Asphalt from the adjoining parking lot crumbled and piled onto the beach. One plan involved reinforcing the lighthouse to let it stand as an island in the advancing sea. In October 1998, Congress appropriated $9.8 million to save this national landmark by moving it to a safer location about a half-mile (0.8 km) inland. The move was accomplished in the summer of 1999 amid much fanfare, and the famous lighthouse stands well protected in its new location—until nature catches up with it again.

Most of South Nags Head, in an inlet-formation zone, was developed since the 1980s and 90s, when all the houses were required to be built a designated distance from the beach. Since then, some oceanfront cottages have been washed away, and the second-tier cottages behind them have become oceanfront, awaiting their turn to topple in. The beach at South Nags Head currently recedes at a rate of 10–16 ft/3–5 m a year. Sandbagging and bulldozing may buy the houses a little more time, but the trade-off is loss of the public beach, debris from ruined homes littering the beach, and septic tanks exposed and broken during each major storm. After septic tanks are repaired and reburied, the houses are sold or rented again.

Farther south, the beach at Rodanthe, the northernmost community on Hatteras Island, erodes at a rate of about 16 ft/4.9 m a year. The house filmed for the 2008 movie *Nights in Rodanthe* was nearly swept into the ocean not long after the movie premiered. The structure was moved to a new lot, then was walloped by Hurricane Bill in August 2009.

Nearly every hurricane that comes through inflicts severe property damage. Extratropical storms, or nor'easters, are more common and last longer, however, and they cause most of the damage along the Outer Banks. Each year, 30 to 40 nor'easters churn up high waves and storm surges in this area.

There are many instances of wild island horses drowning in storms. On September 18, 2003, Hurricane Isabel, a Category 2 storm when it came ashore, descended with record waves nearly 40 ft/12 m high and sustained winds of approximately 85 knots/157 kph. Isabel swept five horses from Carrot Island, off Beaufort, N.C., and carried their bodies 3 mi/5 km east to Harkers Island. Three additional horses survived after they were carried 1 mi/1.6 km south to Shackleford Banks. Between 1989 and 1993, 12 horses died in storms on Assateague Island. The nor'easter of November 2009 that threw tires on the beach at Assateague did not kill any horses, but ripped across the Outer Banks with three days of rain and 40–55 mph/64–89 kph winds. In some places, half to three quarters of the dunes were flattened, and houses were damaged so badly that officials condemned them.

State Highway 12 is a boon to the area, but it has been a costly, and some would say quixotic, venture to maintain a fixed roadway on an unstable island. When sand and water destroy the road, workers rebuild it to the west and stabilize the artificial dunes with bulldozers, sand fencing, sandbags, and grasses. But when a significant storm blows in, the dunes are violated yet again. There are six locations in and near Cape Hatteras NS where the dunes are frequently destroyed by storms. When overwash breaches the dunes, they are usually repaired right away, a practice that interferes with natural barrier overwash processes, potentially increasing vulnerability to storm damage. Government agencies collaborate to fix the dunes to limit the loss of property and maintain access, but holding dunes in place is like holding back the tide—which is in fact another project elsewhere on the island. It may be folly to continue this expensive battle against the elements with no prospect of long-term success; but coastal tourism is economically vital to North Carolina, and the highway is the only vehicular hurricane evacuation route.

Despite more than 75 years of concerted effort to maintain a high, stable artificial dune line on Pea, Hatteras, and Ocracoke islands, the great dunes persistently encroach on the highway with every significant storm. The roads are impassable until the government clears or replaces them. Hurricane Isabel created a new inlet—Isabel Inlet—just north of Hatteras Village, leaving Highway 12 in crumbles on either side. The U.S. Army Corps of Engineers hastily filled the breach before a major flood-tide delta could form. It appears that Hatteras Island would become an archipelago again if left entirely to natural processes.

If Highway 12 is to remain, it must be relocated to the west ahead of the migrating dunes. Building to the west would disrupt fragile wetlands essential to the health of the environment and the missions of two federal agencies. Because erosion has taken its toll, in places the islands are already too narrow to support a new highway. Soon the state will need to build a causeway to carry the road west of the overwash flats or implement a system of water taxis or ferries to move people and vehicles between communities.

It will be hard for state and federal governments to commit funds to a soundside causeway system, but such a project may become politically necessary. Meanwhile, funds for temporary fixes are hemorrhaging from the treasury. Another option is to harmonize with nature and maintain a temporary gravel road across the most vulnerable portions of the island. An unpaved roadway would allow vehicles to pass but would be much easier to repair and relocate when overwashed. And islands with ferry-only access such as Ocracoke, Nantucket, Block Island, and Martha's Vineyard prosper despite lack of a blacktop connection to the mainland.

Ocracoke appears on various 1500s maps as *Wococon*, *Woccocock*, and other similar-sounding variations. This is probably because the name was an Indian word, and it was spelled phonetically by mapmakers who may never have heard the original pronunciation. These gave way to *Occocock*, also spelled various ways) and later to *Ocracoke*.

In 1715, the North Carolina Assembly passed "An Act for Settling and Maintaining Pilots at Roanoke and Ocacock Inlett," but because the land was privately owned at the time, these early settlers were squatters (Stick, 1958). A community originally called Pilot Town flourished along Cockle Creek (the harbor known today as Silver Lake). In 1760, they were allotted 50 acres/20 ha for the settlement, which became Ocracoke Village.

By the end of the colonial period, the only two sizable settlements on the Outer Banks were Ocracoke and Portsmouth. Most ships traveling to and from the major seaports of New Bern, Washington, and Edenton were obliged to pass through Ocracoke inlet, and these two towns stood on either side of it.

Ocracoke Inlet was a major trade route through the Outer Banks, but it was fairly shallow and treacherous, and most ships could not pass through without a pilot. Some large or heavy-laden ships could not pass through it at all.

The first mention of settlement at present-day Portsmouth "on the south side of Ocracoke Inlet" dates to 1685 (Wiss Janney Elstner Associates & John Milner Associates, 2007, p. 15). Portsmouth was founded in 1753 for the purpose of providing a site at Ocracoke Inlet for warehouses and wharves. A gristmill, windmill, and several residences soon followed. By 1770, Portsmouth was the largest settlement on the Outer Banks. Livestock, including horses, roamed this island, too.

Portsmouth became a major port for lightering. Merchants would hire shallow-draft boats, lighters, or barges to carry their goods over the bar or move cargo between ships on opposite sides of the inlet. A town grew up around the inlet, but few wanted to settle there. In 1755, Governor Arthur Dobbs found Portsmouth Harbor "so exposed

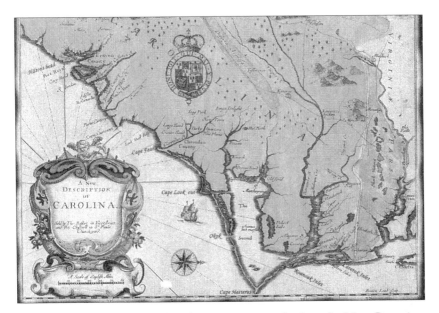

John Speed died in 1629, but his name is attached to the New Description of Carolina (1676). The map, drawn with north to the right, shows several details of the interior, including a desert corresponding roughly to the Sandhills region. Note the spelling of *Ocracoke*—Okok. Oregon Inlet had not been formed yet, and Roanoke Inlet no longer exists. Public domain via Wikimedia Commons.

that every privateer sailing along the coast could from their mast head see every vessel in the harbor, and go in and cut them out, or destroy them" (Olszewski, 1970). Dobbs recommended the construction of a fort on Beacon Island, a 20-acre/8 ha islet west of the inlet in Pamlico Sound. The resulting stronghold, Fort Granville, was garrisoned by 53 officers and men in 1757, but only 5 in 1763. When the Treaty of Paris ended the French and Indian War in 1764, the fort was closed.

In 1789 merchants John Gray Blount and John Wallace established another lightering port on a half-mile-long (0.8 km) aggregate of oyster beds—"Old Rock"—in Ocracoke Inlet. They named the settlement Shell Castle, and in time the surprisingly sturdy base supported wharves, warehouses a windmill, a gristmill, a store, a lumber yard, a lighthouse, and a tavern. Optimally situated to transport goods to and from the mainland, Shell Castle prospered for decades until storm damage and shoaling put the little port out of business around 1812.

The census of 1800 showed that Core Banks—mainly Portsmouth Island and Shell Castle Island—supported a population of 165 whites and 98 blacks, as well as a lumber yard, a tavern, a ship chandlery, a porpoise fishery, and warehouses. In 1841, a marine hospital was built to tend to sick and injured seamen. By 1830, the white population increased to 342, and the slave population had reached 120.

Stock raising was well established on the Outer Banks by the late 1600s. Stick wrote that when Richard Sanderson died in 1733, he owned all of Ocracoke, as well as a large "Stock of Horses, Cattle, Sheep and Hoggs" (1958, p. 33).

In an 1810 letter to the editor of the *Raleigh Star*, an unknown writer describing Portsmouth said,

> Seven years ago an inhabitant of the Island of his own mark, Sheared 700 head of sheep—had between two hundred & fifty, & three hundred head of cattle & near as many horses. . . . It is believed the Island at present is overstocked & much benefit would result from diminution of one third the present number. (Newsome, 1929, p. 401)

A half-century later, Edmund Ruffin pointed out,

> The rearing of horses is a very profitable investment for the small amount of capital required for the business. There are some hundreds of horses, of the dwarfish native breed, on this part of the reef between Portsmouth and Beaufort harbor—ranging at large, and wild, (or untamed,) and continuing the race without any care of their numerous proprietors. (1861, p. 130)

Portsmouth stockmen would attend roundups on Ocracoke, and vice versa, to acquire new horses for their herds. On occasion a Banker Horse sold from Ocracoke to Portsmouth was so eager to return to its herd that it would swim successfully across the inlet. Ocracoke Inlet is a wide, fast-moving stretch of water. Even on a huge ferry burdened with numerous automobiles and passengers, one can feel the powerful grab of current while crossing. Many small boats are incapable of navigating it.

In one well-documented instance, an Ocracoke horse named Old Jerry, who had a taste for straw hats and achieved notoriety by consuming tourists' headgear left within his reach, was sold to someone on Portsmouth Island. Shortly thereafter, he was found grazing contentedly, back on Ocracoke. The horse had swum across 1.5 mi/2.4 km of surging tidal current. A syndicated story about the 1946 Ocracoke pony penning published around the country, in some instances with embellishment, describes a feat even more remarkable, though likely fictional. This version is representative:

It is said that a few years ago a Carteret county man who made a hobby of training the ponies bought a young one at the Ocracoke island penning and bought him to the mainland. . . .

But—it did not like the mainland[.] One night it escaped and was not seen again until his owner revisited the island. There he saw his duly branded pony happily back on his windswept sand bar. To get there the pony had performed an almost incredible feat—he had waded and swum six miles to Shackleford Banks, and after a long walk had crossed Barden Inlet, then after rounding Cape Lookout, had travelled up lonely Core Banks and plunged into Drum inlet. From there he followed the beach to Portsmouth and finally breasted the dangerous currents of Ocracoke inlet, a journey which might have fazed even a well-equipped seafarer. (Munsell, 1946, p. 11)

In 1839, a powerful hurricane inundated Portsmouth and Ocracoke and swept away most of the livestock. In 1846, the same storm that carved both Hatteras and Oregon inlets demolished much of the town. Quoting native pilot Reuben Quidley, Welch wrote in 1885, "there were several families living where the inlet [Hatteras] is now . . . but to their great surprise, in the morning they saw the sea and sound connected together, and the live oaks washing up by the roots and tumbling into the ocean" (pp. 6–7). The new inlet at Hatteras was deeper for a while, so the shipping business that had kept Portsmouth prosperous shifted north. The population of Portsmouth Island declined from 685 in 1860 to 17 in 1956. In 1971 the last two residents moved to the mainland. Today Portsmouth stands as a ghost town, complete with houses, church, U.S. Lifesaving Service station, school, and cemeteries carefully restored by the Park Service. It is listed on the National Register of Historic Places and maintained by the Cape Lookout NS.

The waters surrounding Ocracoke have long been a challenge to sailors. Stick (1958) wrote that during the 16th century, Spanish fleets and Spanish armies swarmed Mexico, Central America, and the Caribbean and transported commodities from the New World along a route that passed near Cape Hatteras on the way to Europe. Ships traveling from Europe to the East Coast colonies shortened the voyage by sailing south to the Canary Islands, riding the Equatorial Current and the Trade Winds to the West Indies, and sailing up the North American coast on the Gulf Stream. Spanish mariners discovered that they could save substantial time in their travels from the Caribbean to Spain if they rode the Gulf Stream current northward along the coast until they were in the vicinity of Cape Hatteras, then headed northeast to cross the Atlantic, aided by the prevailing Westerlies.

Aptly referred to as the Graveyard of the Atlantic, the treacherous Diamond Shoals of Cape Hatteras extend up to 8 mi/13 km into the ocean, far enough that land is often invisible, even in ideal conditions. Many a sailor who believed he was miles out to sea has run on the outer shoals without warning. Strong currents and extreme weather add to the difficulties. Southbound sailing vessels were obliged to hug the coast in order to avoid fighting the Gulf Stream, and sometimes the passage between current and the shoals was only a mile or two (1.6–3.2 km) wide, leaving little margin for error.

In the past few hundred years, there have been more than 1,000 recorded shipwrecks around Cape Hatteras. Even the famous Union ironclad *Monitor* wrecked off Cape Hatteras in a storm. The actual number of losses is probably much higher. Before the 19th century, records were inconsistent and fragmentary. Wrecks became commonplace, and people who could write were not always moved to write about them.

As with many of the Atlantic coastal wild herds, many people believe that the horses that gave rise to Ocracoke's wild herd were shipwreck survivors who swam to the island though stormy seas. Some or all of the foundation animals could have arrived by shipwreck, but as with the other herds, there is no proof. It is clear, however, that ships carrying horses often passed close to the Outer Banks and its dangerous shoals.

Beginning in the mid-1600s, New England was so well supplied with horses, merchants turned a tidy profit exporting them in large numbers to power cane-crushing mills on sugar plantations in the Caribbean and as far away as the Dutch colony of Surinam, in South

The Outer Banks has seen thousands of wrecks. This line engraving was published in *Harper's Weekly* in 1863, depicting the USS *Monitor* sinking in a storm off Cape Hatteras on the night of December 30–31, 1862. Courtesy of the United States Naval History and Heritage Command, #NH 58758 via Wikimedia Commons.

America. Horses could be shipped to Barbados in about 37 days, roughly half the time required for a trip from England. From 1683 to 1794, colonists, mostly in New England, sold over 33,000 horses to Surinam. In fact, Surinam would trade only with vessels that brought horses as part of their cargo.

Merchants realized a 50% profit margin on the sale of horses, or exchanged them for slaves, which they sold to other colonies. Trade was brisk and highly profitable. Logs account for 1,583 horses shipped from Connecticut to Jamaica between 1762 and 1768, but there were apparently many more. Another record counts 27,809 horses and cattle shipped from New London, Connecticut, from 1785 to 1788. In the years 1771 and 1774, 7,130 horses were imported into the British Isles from "North America" (Phillips, 1922, p. 922). Horses were carried on the decks of ships bound for the West Indies. Even Jamaica and Santo Domingo imported horses from New England despite their abundance of livestock. As the planters became wealthy, they began to import elite saddle horses for comfort and prestige, especially Narragansett Pacers from Rhode Island. New England also traded horses to other colonies on the Eastern Seaboard. In 1642 Massachusetts Bay shipped horses to Lord Baltimore's colony in Maryland and in 1665 to Virginia. New England merchants even sold horses to the Dutch living on the Hudson River.

In 1648, Governor John Winthrop of the Massachusetts Bay colony wrote in his journal of a ship "lying before Charlestown [now part of Boston] with eighty horses on board bound for Barbados"—probably an eyewitness account of the first recorded exportation of horses from New England to the West Indies (Phillips, 1922, p. 902). It is also evidenced that New England ships sometimes hugged the coast *en route* to the West Indies. Ships carrying horses could have wrecked anywhere along the way.

Despite patchy records, accounts of equine losses along the Atlantic coast are numerous. During the colonial period, livestock were typically transported on deck, and they often fell victim to storms and rogue waves. On Christmas Day in 1770, a storm struck a small fleet from Connecticut bound for the West Indies and drowned more than 100 horses and a number of sailors. In February 1725, another storm drowned 16 of 18 horses on a sloop from New London and a total of 21 horses on three different Rhode Island ships. In September 1766, a Connecticut vessel bound for Grenada encountered a series of hurricanes that drowned its entire shipment of horses and oxen. The captain sought shelter in Bermuda and saw the bodies of innumerable dead horses floating in the ocean around the island. Another gale on January 7, 1758, struck a vessel in New Haven Harbor awaiting departure to the West Indies. Ten of 34 horses drowned or were battered to death against the rocks. The list of mishaps is long.

Numerous ships carrying horses skirted the Carolina coast, and many horses were lost in maritime disasters. Although it is more likely that the horses of the Outer Banks originated from stockmen who used the islands as a grazing commons, horses fleeing a maritime disaster might have swum to shore and started or contributed to some of the wild herds. Some residents of the Outer Banks may be descendants of shipwreck survivors, and it is possible their horses are, too.

On a gusty November day, the ocean smashes irritably into the beach at Assateague Island, Virginia. Waves this size could drown swimming horses, yet they are minuscule compared to the surf of a violent storm.

Although it is possible for horses to swim to shore from a shipwreck in a stormy sea, the odds are not in their favor. Horses swim with their heads low in the water, and high waves are likely to drown them.

Horses are good swimmers and possess great endurance. One news item ("Battling Stallions," 1951, p. 3B) describes an altercation involving "two or more banker ponies," in which the contenders chased each other "off Ocracoke Island into the waters of Hatteras Inlet, finally swimming through the dangerous current and reaching the safety of Hatteras." In 2012, an Arabian named Air of Temptation demonstrated incredible stamina when he bolted into the ocean at Summerland Beach, California. He swam for *three hours* before he was rescued 1 mi/1.6 km from shore.

Horses do, however, frequently drown when overwhelmed by storm-driven waves, swimming as they do with their heads in or near the water. Near shore, swimming becomes more hazardous as breakers slam them onto sandbars or the beach. There are many accounts of barrier island horses drowning in storm surge, usually in hurricanes but sometimes during minor nor'easters. Most of them were standing on high ground when the surge occurred.

Even if horses managed to make their way to shore from wrecked ships, horses not acclimated to the Banks have often perished, as hardy mustangs introduced to the Chincoteague herd did on Assateague. Edmund Ruffin (1861) commented that horses introduced to Banker herds often succumbed to the harsh conditions and the poor-quality forage.

Any genes contributed to the herds by shipwreck survivors would have been very similar to those of the horses that safely arrived by other means. The horses traveling along Atlantic shipping routes were the same horses found in the colonies: Spanish Jennets; English, Dutch, Irish, and French horses; and the horses developed in the colonies through the interbreeding of these types.

Stud books, newspaper articles, and stallion advertisements from the 16th, 17th, and 18th centuries give insight into the breeds that were popular in the colonies. Wallace found that the horses of colonial Virginia, Pennsylvania, and Maryland were similar in size and type because of "constant intercourse and trade" among those colonies (1897, p. 141).

The earliest farm animals in the English colonies of North America were probably Spanish livestock bought (or, by some accounts, stolen) from the Spanish ranches in the Caribbean. Records are vague, incomplete, and confusing—at the time, writers often used the term "cattle" to mean any livestock. In 1609, six or seven ships from England brought many domestic animals to Jamestown, including a stallion and six mares, presumably Spanish horses from the Caribbean. But during the "starving time" the following winter, the colonists butchered them all for food. Thomas Dale brought 17 horses, probably Spanish, in 1611; Samuel Argall obtained French horses in a raid on Nova Scotia in 1613; and the Virginia Company supplied English horses in the 1620s. Some of these horses, their descendants, and later imports seem to have avoided the cookpot.

The next wave of livestock appears to have originated in Europe. In 1625, the Dutch West India Company shipped horses from the Netherlands to New York, and in 1635 Dutch draft horses arrived in the form of 27 Flanders mares and three stallions. Francis Higginson shipped about 50 mares and stallions to Massachusetts Bay, perhaps from Leicestershire, in 1629; but most died *en route* or shortly after, and only one stallion and seven mares survived.

Swedes settled southeastern Pennsylvania with their Old World horses, which were "undoubtedly pacers" (Phillips, 1922, p. 904). New Jersey acquired horses not from Europe, but from New York, Pennsylvania, and Virginia, and, like other colonies, allowed them to forage free range. By the mid-1600s, Connecticut and Massachusetts supported enormous herds of free-roaming horses, which increased faster than traders could sell them to the West Indies. By the 1700s the other colonies were in similar straits. Phillips (1922, p. 903) quotes William Harris, who had been sent out by the Board of Trade in 1675, and observed that the country had so many horses "that men know not what to do with them."

Phillips (1922, pp. 894–895) wrote,

> In view of the lack of any direct evidence to the contrary, it is fair to assume that the first shipments were mainly from England and of the small nondescript type which at that time made up the bulk of the English horses. There was, however, some admixture of other blood. In the primary importation into the Massachusetts Bay colony in 1629, three at least are mentioned specifically as "having come out of Leicestershire," which at that time was the source of a more or less distinct type of horse of a sort better than the average. The importation of Flemish mares also has been noted. Wallace contends that these latter were not Flemish but were rather of a Dutch type, but his conclusion is based merely on the fact that the vessel cleared from a Dutch port—which does not seem a very valid reason for controverting Winthrop's specific statement as to their Flemish origin, especially since Flemish horses were well known at that period as a distinct type.
>
> There is one other possible source of some of the New England horses which deserves consideration, especially because it may tend to explain in some measure the persistently small

size of these horses, even when carefully bred—as later they were in Rhode Island and Connecticut—and, further, the constant occurrence among them of individuals possessed of a natural pacing gait. This possible progenitor is to be found in the Irish hobbies, a race of small, hardy, wild ponies existing in Ireland during the first part of the 17th century. These horses were in great demand in England for saddle purposes, and were exported thence in such quantities that they are said to have become practically extinct in Ireland before the year 1634. They were well known in England, and their natural pacing gait made them especially desirable in any place where travel was of necessity on horseback; it is not at all improbable, therefore, that some of them found their way to New England, where they would have been especially serviceable. There seems to be no direct evidence to this effect, but any comparison of such fragmentary descriptions of the two as are available discloses a rather striking similarity between these Irish hobbies and the famous Narragansett pacers which were later developed in Rhode Island.

In colonial times, horses were not categorized as breeds, but rather types or families recognized by one progenitor (such as Snip) or an owner's name (for example, The Godolphin Arabian, Byerley Turk, Justin Morgan). These horses were grouped primarily by ability, usefulness, and individual accomplishment, and from these sires and mares arose may diverse types that evolved into what we now know as breeds.

The Narragansett Pacer of Rhode Island was the first unique American breed. It was probably developed from English, Irish, Spanish, and Dutch horses imported in the early 1600s. The Galloway, the rugged little pacing horse of Scotland, probably figured prominently in its heritage. William Robinson, the Lieutenant Governor of Rhode Island, improved the lines by importing a stallion named Snip, who was variously described in writings of the time as an Andalusian, a Thoroughbred, a Barb, and an Arabian. The Hazard family of Rhode Island), who inherited Robinson's estate, maintains that Snip was a fine Spanish stallion that Robinson imported directly from Andalusia.

The Narragansett Pacer quickly became popular throughout colonial America. Also known as "Rhode Islands" or "New England Pacing

Horses," this breed was present in South Carolina as early as 1682 and probably in North Carolina, Virginia, and Maryland around the same time. Narragansetts probably reached North Carolina not only by trade, but also with immigrants from New England, for example, "Quakers from Newport, Rhode Island, who had settled in the Albemarle region of North Carolina by 1700, then gradually spread into the counties south of Albemarle Sound" (Little, 2012, p. 18). However Narragansetts arrived, they were the dominant saddle horse until the early 1740s, when the Colonial Spanish-blooded Chickasaw (or Choctaw) surpassed it in popularity.

Early mainland roads were poor, little more than paths through the forest. The Narragansett Pacer was a fast, sure-footed horse with an uncommonly smooth gait and great endurance, making it possible for the rider to comfortably travel the many miles between communities. He could pace 12–14 mph and could sustain that speed without undue fatigue to either himself or his rider. A Narragansett Pacer could carry a man on a journey of 800 miles at 100 miles per day. During the 1700s, colonists prized these horses and bred large numbers of them. Newspaper advertisements for stud service from around the turn of the 19th century used descriptions such as "stout and handsome"; "high-spirited . . . and perfectly sure-footed"; "a chestnut colour, inclined to a sorrel, 14 hands 3 inches high, round made, and very strong"; and "tractable, and free from vicious habits" (Harrison, 1931, pp. 163–164).

James Fenimore Cooper described the Narragansett Pacer in a footnote to the second edition of *The Last of the Mohicans* that reads, in part,

> They were small, commonly of the colour called sorrel in America, and distinguished by their habit of pacing. Horses of this race were, and are still, in much request as saddle horses, on account of their hardiness and the ease of their movements. As they were also sure of foot, the Narragansets were greatly sought for by females who were obliged to travel over the roots and holes in the 'new countries.' (1831, p. 14)

Phillips (1922, p. 926) quotes an article by Robert Livingston of New York from the 1832 edition of the *Edinburgh Encyclopedia*:

> They have handsome foreheads, the head clean, the neck long, the arms and legs thin and taper; the hindquarters are narrow

and the hocks a little crooked, which is here called sickle hocked, which turns the hind feet out a little: their color is generally, though not always, bright sorrel; they are very spirited and carry both head and tail high. But what is most remarkable is that they amble with more speed than most horses trot, so that it is difficult to put some of them upon a gallop. Notwithstanding this facility of ambling, where the ground, requires it, as when the roads are rough and stony, they have a fine easy single footed trot. These circumstances, together with their being very sure footed, render them the finest saddle horses in the world; they neither fatigue themselves nor their rider. It is generally to be lamented that this invaluable breed of horses is now almost lost by being mixed with those imported from England and from other parts of the United States.

In Virginia, breeders crossed the Narragansett, English Thoroughbreds, and Chickasaw horses. Horsemen also imported Scottish Galloways and Irish Hobbies to Virginia from England or from the New England states. Many of the horses of Colonial Virginia could pace, but they were smaller and usually capable of trotting and cantering. Wallace wrote:

When the Rev. Dr. McSparran, of Rhode Island, made a trip in Virginia and rode the Virginia pacers some hundreds of miles, early in the last [18th] century, he seems to have observed them closely and spoke very highly of them, but he said they were not so large and strong as the Narragansett's, nor so easy and gliding in their action. It might be suggested that this opinion was the natural result of esteeming one's own as better than those of a neighbor, but he was certainly right in the matter of size. In 1768 the Rhode Island horses averaged fourteen hands one inch, while the Virginia horses averaged (1750–52) thirteen hands one and three-quarter inches, making a difference of three and one-quarter inches in height. In the matter of gait they were not all natural pacers. . . . From this it may be inferred that breeders, in order to increase the size, had incorporated more or less of the blood of the early Dutch importations (1897, p. 134).

Through much of the 18th century, "nothing was accepted as a 'saddle horse' that could not take the pacing gait and its various modifications" (Wallace, 1897, p. 115). But as roads improved, Americans came to prefer horse-drawn conveyances to riding astride and favored trotters as carriage animals. Breeders lost interest in the Narragansett Pacer; Herbert described the breed as "extinct" (1857, p. 112) before the Civil War. Wallace wrote:

> After more than a hundred years of faithful service, of great popularity, and of profitable returns to their breeders, the little Narragansetts began to disappear, just as their ancestors had disappeared a century earlier. Rhode Island was no longer a frontier settlement, but had grown into a rich and prosperous State. Mere bridle paths through the woods had developed into broad, smooth highways, and wheeled vehicles had taken the place of the saddle. Under these changed conditions, the little pacer was no longer desirable or even tolerable as a harness horse, and he was supplanted by a larger and more stylish type of horse, better suited to the particular kind of work required of him. This was simply the "survival of the fittest," considering the nature of the services required of the animal (1897, p. 182).

The pacers of the American colonies were popular for long-distance travel, sport, and general use. Spanish planters in the West Indies, notably Cuba, paid premium prices for the Narragansett Pacers, stocking their stables with the most valuable and elite examples of the breed. In so doing, they depleted the nursery until they grew scarce, and suppliers in Rhode Island were breeding fewer every year. Eventually the breed collapsed.

As the Narragansett Pacer faded into obscurity, the Spanish horse moved into the limelight. D. Phillip Sponenberg, DVM, PhD, a professor at the Virginia-Maryland Regional College of Veterinary Medicine, noted that the earliest Spanish horses imported to North America, including the populations in the southeastern United States, were typically brought from Mexico rather than directly from the Caribbean (Sponenberg, 1992). After these original introductions, it was uncommon for planters to import horses directly from Spain to cross into these local populations. In South America, however, the earliest horses were introduced from the Antilles, followed by repeated importations of horses from the Caribbean and directly from Spain (Sponenberg, 1992). This divergence of bloodlines gave rise to the numerous distinct types of pure Colonial Spanish Horse that persist today.

Around 1700, the purely Spanish horse was found in an arch that stretched northward from Florida; through the Carolinas, Tennessee, and the Great Plains; and into the Western mountains. These horses averaged just under 13.2 hands, and many were gaited—able to amble, pace, trot, and canter.

By the mid-1700s, great numbers of untended Spanish horses roamed the Southeast, the descendants of Jennets introduced by Spanish explorers, probably after 1580. The first Europeans to settle the Carolina mountains found large numbers of wild horses roaming the open forests. Native American tribes, both Western and Eastern, acquired Spanish Jennets by trading with or stealing from European settlers or by capturing feral animals.

In the 18th century, two strains of Spanish horse were common along the Atlantic Seaboard—the Seminole or Creek horse originating in Florida, "small in size and capricious in nature," and the Choctaw or Chickasaw horse, "larger and more docile," originating in the plains west of the Mississippi River (Harrison, 1931, p. 170). These types persist in Colonial Spanish horses today. Steve Edwards (2010), a breeder of Colonial Spanish horses, observed that some Banker stallions, like the legendary Red Feather, are smaller and more aggressive, often amassing large herds of mares by virtue of their superior fighting ability. The larger stallions, like his adopted Croatoan, tend to be calm and very easy to train.

Smyth (1784, p. 139) described the Chickasaw horses as "named from a nation of Indians who are very careful in preserving a fine breed of Spanish horses they have long possessed, unmixed with any other." This stock was widely distributed and bred along the Atlantic Seaboard throughout the 18th century.

In time, a wide variety of Indian horses were termed "Chickasaws." Harrison (1931, pp. 167–168) commented on the blurring of distinctions:

> At the end of the eighteenth century the name "Chickasaw" had spread north from Carolina to connote, if not a breed, a *type* of desirable saddle horse derived from Spanish America.

Along the Atlantic Seaboard, purely Spanish horses occurred in two distinct types—the Seminole or Creek horse originating in Florida, "small in size and capricious in nature," and the Chickasaw or Choctaw horse, "larger and more docile," originating in the plains west of the Mississippi River (Harrison, 1931, p. 170). The Corolla Banker herd shows evidence of both lineages.

> John Davis and other travelers heard and recorded the name as then current in Virginia and Maryland in the same sense that the name 'mustang' was later used.

As evidence he quotes an interesting 1801 stud advertisement from Norfolk, Va., that refers to Spot, a "pure Chickasaw horse. . . . brought from South America" (p. 168).

In the early 19th century David Ramsay, physician, public official, and prominent historian of the American Revolution, apparently referred to all Spanish-blooded horses as Chickasaws when he wrote,

> Before the year 1754 the best horses for the draught or saddle in Carolina were called the Chickesaw breed. These were originally introduced by the Spaniards into Florida, and in the course of time had astonishingly increased. Great numbers ranged wild. . . . Many of them were caught and tamed by the Indians, and sold to the traders. They made use of them for pack horses to bring their peltry to market, and afterwards sold them in the low country. These horses in general were handsome, active, and hardy, but small; seldom exceeding thirteen hands and a half in height. The mares in

particular, when crossed with English blooded horses, produced colts of great beauty, strength and swiftness. Before the year 1754 these Chickesaw horses were the favorite breed. (1809, p. 403)

Until the mid-18th century, wealthy planters typically invested in expensive pacers, while poor subsistence farmers acquired Spanish ponies that Indians conveyed from the south and west to traders in Virginia and Carolina.

Harrison (1931, p. 168) wrote,

[T]he contemporary evidence is that early in the eighteenth century the Carolina planters, wedded to the comforts of the Narragansett pacer, despised the pack horses brought in by the Indian traders as 'tackies'. There is no evidence at all that they esteemed any Indian horse as fit for the saddle and turf until after 1740.

Before 1740, traders would frequently sell the little Indian horses to poor farmers. Lowland stockmen used the local islands and necks as pastures, and freed their horses to graze the marshes and prodigiously increase their numbers. The free-roaming horses on barrier islands in North and South Carolina and Georgia were termed "Marsh Tackies," though it is unclear whether this term was used dismissively by the social elite or to denote Spanish Chickasaw heritage.

In 1922, Hervey Allen immortalized the lineage of these hardy little horses in his poem "Marsh Tackies" (Heyward & Allen, 1922, pp. 112–113).

Browsing on the salty marsh grass,
Barrel-ribbed and blowsy-bellied,
With a neigh as shrill as whistles
And their mouths red-raw from thistles,
I have seen the brown marsh tackies,
Hiding in the swamps at Kiawah,
With the gray mosquito patches
Gory on their shaggy thatches.

Balky, vicious, and degenerates,
They are small as Spanish jennets,
But their sires were with El Tarab,

A Native American (Plains) woman rides a Spanish horse while her two children travel in a wooden cage on a travois, *circa* 1870–1900. Photographer unknown. Public domain, via Wikimedia Commons.

When he conquered Andalusia
For the Prophet and the Arab;
And they came with Ponce de Leon,
When the Spaniard made a peon
And a Christian of the Carib.
Peering from palmetto thickets
At some fort's coquina wickets,
Startled Indians saw them grazing,
Thunder-stamping and amazing
As the beasts from other stars,
When they galloped down savannas,
And their masters seemed centaurs
With the new white metal blazing.

Thus they came, these little beasts,
With the men-at-arms and priests,
In the west with Coronado
When he reached the Colorado,
In the east with bold De Soto

In the search for El Dorado,

And they packed the bells and toys
That the chieftains loved like boys;
Struggling through the swamps and briars
After dons and tonsured friars;
Dying in the forests dismal,
Till the shrill of silver clarion
Brought the buzzards to the carrion
Round the smoke of lonely fires
In a continent abysmal.

So De Soto left them dying,
Heedless of their human crying;
Here he turned them loose to die
Underneath a foreign sky;
But they lived on thicket dross,
On the leaves and Spanish moss—
And I wonder, and I wonder,
When I hear the startled thunder
Of their hoofs die down the reaches
Of these Carolina beaches.

Despite the widespread prejudice against small horses and those ridden by Indians, Spanish horses quickly garnered respect among horsemen. Men would show up at match races with nondescript Spanish horses and best the competition again and again, stealing purses from under the noses of elite Thoroughbreds. Southern breeders soon began crossing readily available native Spanish horses with expensive imports. Harrison observed (1931, p. 55) that "the longest Carolina racehorse pedigrees all extend to a taproot in the Chickasaw stock." Even in New York and New England, which esteemed English, French, and Dutch horses, breeders used North American Spanish horses to improve bloodlines.

Wallace (1897, p.114) lamented the lack of detailed information about native Spanish horses, but offered his own impressions:

> We here have a stock of horses that the people of Virginia
> have bred and ridden and raced for a hundred years, and

Racing Marsh Tackies on the beach was once a winter tradition, following the fall harvest. Carolina Marsh Tackies persist as a rare, historic breed. In 2012, 17 raced before a crowd of more than 7,000 spectators on Coligny Beach, Hilton Head, SC. Photograph by Anthony Surbeck via Wikimedia Commons.

we know comparatively nothing about them. They seem to have been specially adapted to the saddle, but they could run four miles, or they could run a quarter of a mile, like an arrow from a bow. They were not a breed, although selecting and crossing and interbreeding for a hundred years would make them quite homogeneous. There is a romantic interest attaching to these little horses . . . this old stock furnished half the foundation, in a vast majority of cases, for the triumphs of future generations of the Virginia race horse, and the same may be said of the old English stock upon which the eastern blood was engrafted.

Culver (1922, p. 39) also made note of the homogeneity of "Chickashaw" [sic] horses in the Carolinas prior to 1754 and the scarcity of imported stock during that period. He described the horse as "of small size but well formed and active, and when covered with imported thoroughbreds produced animals of great beauty, strength and speed."

The Spanish horse persisted in the Seminole and Chickasaw strains well into the 18th century. In the new British colony of East Florida, novelist and playwright Oliver Goldsmith (or his brother John) described the local horses as "of the Spanish breed, of great spirit, but little strength; they are seldom above fourteen hands high: the Indians here, by mixing the Spanish breed with the Carolina, have excellent horses, both for service and beauty" (1768, p. 361).

In most of colonial America, horse racing had always been popular for sport and status. By 1748, races at the pace, trot, and gallop had become so commonplace in New Jersey colony, racing was outlawed as a public nuisance. Then, as now, fine horses were viewed as status symbols. Men of the upper class talked about their horses and admired them in the same way that they would themselves or one another. As colonists became more prosperous, they imported English Thoroughbreds and Arabians to increase the size, speed, and quality of Colonial horses and matched them over 6-mi/9.7-km courses or in three to five 4-mi/6.4-km heats.

The American Quarter Horse originated in the Carolinas and Virginia. Early settlers found Virginia and the Carolinas covered with old-growth forest. Cleared land represented an enormous investment in time and sweat and was necessary for agriculture. Unable to spare the valuable cleared land for racetracks, people who lived in heavily forested regions raced horses in pairs along parallel quarter-mile (0.4-km) tracks hewn through the woods, often separated by trees or a fence. Until around the time of the Civil War, horse racing was the primary American sport, and outcomes often involved civic pride in addition to personal wealth.

Smyth (1784, pp. 22–23) described the early quarter racing horse as running

> with astonishing velocity, beating every other, for that distance, with great ease; but they have no bottom. However, I am confident that there is not a horse in England, nor perhaps the whole world, that can excel them in rapid speed: and these likewise make excellent saddle horses for the road.
>
> The Virginians, of all ranks and denominations, are excessively fond of horses, and especially those of the race breed. The gentlemen of fortune expend great sums on their studs, generally keeping handsome carriages, and several elegant sets of horses, as well as others for the race and road: even the most indigent person has his saddle-horse, which he rides to every place, and on every occasion; for in this country nobody walks on foot the smallest distance. . . . In short, their horses are their pleasure, and their pride.

From 1682 to 1740, the Narragansett Pacer was the dominant breed in the Carolinas; from 1740 to 1786, the Chickasaw; and from

1755 onward, horses descending from English stock. Colonists had an ardent enthusiasm for fast horses, and as their fortunes grew, they began to import English Thoroughbred and Arabian horses from Europe. Samuel Patton and Samuel Gist imported Bulle Rock, an esteemed son of the Darley Arabian and grandson of the Byerley Turk (two of the three primary foundation sires of the American Thoroughbred) to Virginia in 1730 at the age of 21, and offered him at stud to local mares. His English owner noted that the American colonies were passionate about quarter-racing on Chickasaw horses and correctly speculated that they would enthusiastically bring their mares to an English Thoroughbred. Bulle Rock was the first of many European and Middle Eastern race horses imported to "improve" the existing gene pool in hopes of producing faster, larger horses. Despite arriving in America late in life, Bulle Rock was probably the first stallion who could have been described as a leading sire in the Colonies.

Wallace (1897, pp. 116–117) explained,

> From about 1750 to 1770 seems to have been a period of great prosperity in Virginia and, notwithstanding the general improvidence of the times, many of the large landholders and planters were getting rich from their fine crops of tobacco and their Negroes. This prosperity manifested itself strongly in the direction of the popular sport of horse racing and improving the size, quality, and fleetness of the running horse. England had then been selecting, importing Eastern blood, and "breeding to the winner" for a hundred years, with more or less intelligence and success, while the colonists had rested content with the descendants of the first importations from the mother country.

The fervor for imported racing stock took hold first in Virginia and Maryland and spread to the Carolinas by around 1754. Many of these English Thoroughbreds were stallions who stood at stud in Virginia and the Carolinas. The historical record is shaped by the snobbery of the upper class—the blooded stallions were advertised and celebrated, while the local mares were scarcely acknowledged.

Mares are vital to any horse breeding operation. Clearly, the dam provides 50% of the foal's genes and 100% of its environment during gestation, as well as strong influence in shaping the mind and body of a young foal. Themselves a product of a sexist culture that favored males, however, horsemen of the time concluded that stallions made a far greater genetic contribution and often regarded mares as little more than carriers for the get of a sire. Moreover, a mare crossed with an inferior horse was somehow tainted, and thereafter incapable of producing a "pure" foal:

> A mare once crossed with a sire of different blood, not only produces, but *becomes* herself, a cross; and is incapable of ever again producing her own strain. Thus a thorough mare, once stinted to a coldblooded horse, could never again bear the pure colt, even to a pure sire; while a cold-blooded mare, having once foaled to a thorough horse, would always be improved as a breeder by the change produced in her own constitution. (Herbert, 1857, p. 113)

While much was written about Thoroughbred sires, the mares they served often faded into obscurity. The majority were probably Spanish or Spanish crosses. Some of them bore piebald or skewbald coats, which Harrison says were "a characteristic of the plains horses, as noted in 1804 by Lewis & Clark" (1934, p. 39). Apparently some had Appaloosa markings as well. Harrison wrote (1934, p. 39), that in the late 18th century "the quarter racing 'Chickasaw' or 'Opelousas' stock still abounded in the Roanoke valley." Elsewhere he notes, "there were a number of mares 'from Old Spain' in Virginia and Maryland before 1750" and "for some generations prior to 1750 Virginia and Maryland had absorbed a steady inflow of mares 'from New Spain,' brought back by [I]ndian traders, from their contacts with the horse owning [I]ndians of the Southwest" (1929, p. 23).

Before 1730 the horses of the English colonies were either Spanish-blooded Chickasaw stock or descendants of horses imported from Spain and Spanish colonies, England, France, or the Netherlands. The Indian ponies of the West descended directly from the earliest Spanish horses. But through the 1700s the East Coast Spanish horses were crossed with Narragansett Pacers, English Thoroughbreds, heavy French and Dutch draft horses, and Andalusian horses of a more modern derivation.

In 1747, Samuel Ogle, the resident lieutenant governor of Maryland, imported Spanish, Barb, and Arabian horses to his Belair Stud, the first prominent stud in America. Another renowned breeding

Frederic Remington (1895) depicted Florida Cracker Cowboys and Cracker Horses on canvas. Courtesy of Cornell University Library, Making of America Digital Collection.

facility, John's Island Stud, was established in South Carolina in 1750 by Edward Fenwick. The founder of the South Carolina Jockey Club at Charleston in 1758, Fenwick imported many descendants of the Godolphin Arabian and often crossed them with Chickasaw Spanish ponies.

The Thoroughbred gained popularity as a racehorse, especially among the social elite, and upper-class horsemen came to regard this breed as the *only* horse breed of exceptional quality. Wealthy breeders considered quarter racing a primitive sport fit only for frontiersmen and incorrectly concluded that the small Spanish horses raced at that distance because they had no "bottom" or endurance. Thoroughbreds were raced on 3-or 4-mile tracks, requiring both speed and stamina to win.

As with most breeds, the exact origins of the Quarter Horse are open to speculation. One of the foundation sires was Janus, an English Thoroughbred imported to Virginia as a 10-year-old in 1746. All modern Thoroughbreds can trace their lineage to at least one of three foundation stallions of Arabian, Barb, and Turkoman heritage imported into England from the Middle East: the Byerley Turk (1689), the Darley Arabian (1703), and the Godolphin Arabian (1729). Janus, a grandson of the Godolphin Arabian, stood at stud for 24 years in North Carolina and southern Virginia. Janus was not built like today's Thoroughbred or even a modern Quarter Horse, but was a compact, muscular 14.1 hands (57 in. /1.45 m) tall, "a small but beautiful horse. . . . chestnut; speckled on the rump as he grew old; a small blaze in the face, and hind foot white" ("D.," 1832, p. 272). Wallace (1897, p. 95) observed, "Janus became the progenitor of a tribe of very fast quarter horses, and although he did not found that tribe, which had been in existence for a hundred years on the border line between Virginia and North Carolina, he doubtless improved it."

Theodore Dodge (1892, p. 671) observed that horse breeding in the American colonies was often a haphazard affair:

A farmer had a stanch mare. The only available stallion was in the neighboring village—perhaps on circuit. All he could see was that there were good qualities present in both, and he believed that these would be transmitted. . . . Often the mare was not bred from until she was unfitted for work by something which equally unfitted her for breeding. No doubt the average produce of this lack of method may have been of excellent service in its way, but it was none the less "nondescript."

Colonial Spanish horses were used for riding, driving, and draft. When taller, heavier horses gained popularity, the cobby Spanish horse fell out of fashion and its numbers rapidly decreased. Racism also played a role in its loss of popularity. The small, stocky Spanish horse was associated with Indians, Mexicans, and the poor, and because of this association was perceived as lower in quality than the larger breeds of the dominant English culture. In the late 1800s, Spanish Indian ponies were systematically exterminated by order of the U.S. government in an effort to demoralize and subjugate the native people. The once-ubiquitous Spanish horse was suddenly teetering on the brink of extinction.

Numerous lines of Colonial Spanish horses descend from old Spanish bloodlines, and, according to Sponenberg, "are a direct remnant of the Iberian horses of the 1500s" (1992, p. 335). The Colonial Spanish horse strains of today include the Banker, the Belsky,

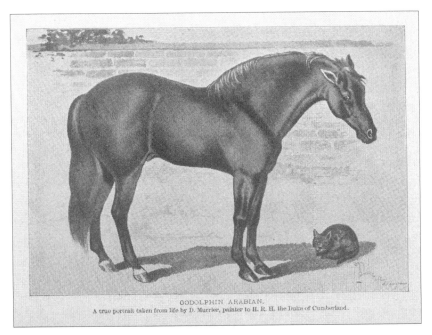

GODOLPHIN ARABIAN.
A true portrait taken from life by D. Murrier, painter to H. R. H. the Duke of Cumberland.

The Godolphin Arabian (*circa* 1724–1753), was one of three sires that founded the Thoroughbred horse. He was foaled in Yemen, then given as a gift to Louis XV of France in 1730. He was imported to England, and at the time was not considered a suitable prospect for stud. He was only 15 hands, and larger horses were the fashion in Europe. When a mare named Roxana was brought to the stud for service to a prized stallion named Hobgoblin, she refused to breed him, and stood for the Godolphin Arabian instead. This interlude produced a swift colt named Lath, who won the Queen's Plate nine times in nine starts at the Newmarket races. Thereafter, the Arabian was the Earl of Godolphin's prize stallion. Every Thoroughbred alive today traces his lineage back to him, usually along many branches of its family tree. Painting by D. Murrier, via Wikimedia Commons.

the Cerbat, the Choctaw, the Florida Cracker, the Marsh Tacky, the New Mexico, the Santa Cruz, the Sulphur, the Wilbur-Cruce, and some strains of the Pryor Mountain. All these breeds are classed as critically endangered, both collectively and individually. There are numerous breed registries for horses of the Colonial Spanish type: Spanish Mustang Registry, Spanish Barb Breeders Association, Southwest; Spanish Mustang Association, Florida Cracker Horse Association, and American Indian Horse Registry. Each of these strains is similar to the others, but each registry emphasizes different characteristics. The Horse of the Americas registry accepts all Colonial Spanish strains. Sponenberg says that it is important to conserve these North American horses of old Spanish bloodlines "since they probably most closely represent the original, less selected type of Iberian horse brought to the New World" (1992, p. 337).

Sponenberg writes (1992) that through centuries of divergent selection, the modern Iberian Spanish horse is quite different from the ancient Jennet, and certain New World Spanish breeds are closer in type to the historic horse of the Golden Age of Spain. He points out (2011) that the old Spanish horse type was variable. Some individuals were compact and heavy, and others were lightly built. Some horses had higher- or lower-set tails or broader or narrower chests. Ryden (2005) writes that Roman-nosed Barb-type and dished-faced Arabian-type individuals often can be found within in the same herd of Spanish-blooded mustangs. These differences are observable in Banker horses. When overfed in domesticity, Bankers typically develop a cobby, pony-like appearance with fat over the neck, back, and hindquarters that obscures the lines of Spanish conformation.

There is great disagreement about which breed is the most direct descendant of the original Spanish Jennet. Andalusians, Lusitanos, Lipizzaners, Cerbat and Pryor Mountain Mustangs, Paso Finos, Peruvian Pasos, and the free-roaming horses of the Banks all descend from Spanish stock; but that blood has mixed, lines have diverged, and all have developed into unique breeds.

In 2007, inspectors from the Horse of the Americas breed registry evaluated the conformation of Corolla and Shackleford Banks horses. They found that all the horses of both herds had the conformation, gaits, and skeletal structure of Colonial Spanish Horses. Banker Horses are accepted by the Horse of the Americas registry as Colonial Spanish horses based on their physical characteristics, even though their origins are obscure.

In the 1970s, certain members of the Ocracoke herd were admitted to the Spanish Mustang Registry as purebreds, and in 1982, two Shackleford horses were admitted. There have been no further inclusions from East Coast feral populations. Some present-day Ocracoke horses, however, descend from an Andalusian stallion outcrossed into the herd in the 1970s. Andalusians are of Spanish heritage, but are a different breed entirely. The Ocracoke horses resulting from these

Lakota Warchief Rain in the Face astride a colonial Spanish horse, *circa* 1876, the year he participated in the Battle of Little Big Horn. Photographer unknown. Public domain, via Wikimedia Commons.

matings are regarded as crossbreeds; as such, the Spanish Mustang Registry considered them ineligible for registration.

Breeds persist for as long as people esteem their unique qualities, or, in the case of some wild herds, when people stop interfering with them. When a breed is repeatedly crossbred with outside horses, it loses its distinctiveness. Breeds become extinct when they are no longer valued, when their performance niche becomes obsolete, or when another breed becomes better at the job for which they were bred. At least 107 equine breeds are known to have become extinct.

E. Gus Cothran of Texas A&M University has studied the DNA in blood samples from horses all over the globe and has offered insights on the relationship of Banker Horses to other breeds. His work provides a scientific basis for discussing the origins of these horses. He says that Corolla horses are a unique population with low genetic variability—only 29 alleles—and show no close resemblance to any

Colonial Spanish Horse Type Matrix

	Most typical—score 1	Least typical—score 5
Head Profile	Concave/flat on forehead and then convex from top of nasal area to top of upper lip (subconvex) OR Uniformly slightly convex from poll to muzzle OR Straight	Dished as in Arabian OR Markedly convex
Head Front View	Wide between eyes (cranial portion), but tapering and "chiseled" in nasal/facial portion (A very important indicator, and width between eyes with sculpted taper to fine muzzle is very typical.)	Wide and fleshy throughout head from cranial portion to muzzle
Nostrils	Small, thin, crescent-shaped; flare larger when excited or exerting	Large, round, and open at rest
Ears	Small to medium length with distinctive notch or inward point at tips	Long, straight, with no inward point at tip OR thick, wide, or boxy
Eyes	Vary from large to small (pig eyes); usually fairly high on head	Large and bold, low on head
Muzzle Profile	Refined, usually with the top lip longer than the bottom lip	Coarse and thick with lower lip loose, large, and projecting beyond upper lip
Muzzle Front View	Fine taper down face to nostrils, slight outward flare, and then inward delicate curve to small, fine muzzle that is narrower than region between nostrils	Coarse and rounded OR heavy and somewhat square as the Quarter Horses, rather than having the tapering curves of the typical muzzle
Neck	Wide from side, sometimes ewe-necked, attached low on chest	Thin, long, and set high on chest
Height	Usually 13.2–14.2 hands (54–58 in./1.37–1.47 m) high; horses over 15 hands (60 in./1.53 m) are not typical	Under 13 hands (52 in./1.32 m) or over 15 hands (60 in./1.53 m)
Withers	Pronounced and obvious—"sharp"	Low, thick, and meaty
Back	Short, strong	Long, weak, and plain
Croup	Angled from top to tail. Usually a 30° slope, some are steeper.	Flat or high

Adapted from Sponenberg and Reed (2009, pp. 140–142).

	Most typical—score 1	Least typical—score 5
Tail Set	Low; tail follows the croup angle so that tail "falls off" the croup	High; tail up above the angle of the croup
Shoulder	Should be long and 45–55°	Short and steeper than 55°
Chest Profile	Deep, usually accounting for half of height	Shallow, less than half of height
Chest Front View	Narrow and "pointed" in an "A" shape	Broad with chest flat across
Chestnuts	Small, frequently absent on rear, and flat rather than thick	Large and thick
Rear Limbs Rear View	Straight along whole length OR inward to have close hocks and then straight to ground ("close hocks") OR slightly turned out from hocks to ground ("cow hocks"), but not extreme. Legs very flexible. At trot the hind track often lands past the front track.	Excessive "cow hocks." Heavy, bunchy gaskin muscle, tight tendons.
Feathering on Legs	Absent to light fetlock feathering, though some have long silky hair above ergot and a "comb" of curled hair up back of cannon. Some horses from mountain areas have more feathering than others and lose this after moving to other environments.	Coarse, abundant feathering as is seen in some draft horse breeds
Rear	Contour from top of croup to gaskin has a "break" in line at the point of the butt	Contour from top of croup to gaskin is full and round ("apple butt") with no break at the point of the butt
Hip Rear View	Spine higher than hip, resulting in "rafter" hip Usually no crease from heavy muscling	Thickly muscled with a distinct crease down the rear
Hip Profile	Long and sloping, well angled, and not heavy	Short, poorly angled
Muscling	Long and tapered	Short and thick ("bunchy")
Front Cannon Bones	Cross-section is round (Best to palpate this below the splint bones.)	Cross-section is flat across the rear of the bone

Unmistakable Spanish conformation is evident in the horses of the Outer Banks, such as this Shackleford Banks stallion . . .

known horse breed. This lack of diversity is probably the result of genetic loss caused by a shrinking breeding population. This analysis indicates that they have bred only to each other for quite some time, to the point of inbreeding. He wrote. "Rather than being feral horses with a mixture of domestic breeds, they are in effect a breed unto themselves" (Ives, 2007, p. 13).

The horses of the North Carolina coast—Corolla, Shackleford Banks, Carrot Island, and Ocracoke—have more genetically in common with one another than with other breeds. Shared ancestry could mean that they descended from a single population that was placed on the island or arrived by shipwreck. Conversely, it could indicate that each herd originated from horses on the nearby mainland that were then of similar type and breeding. Their genes and conformation show Spanish ancestry, but do not clarify just what that ancestry was or when and how ancestors arrived on the islands.

Cothran (personal communication, April 20, 2011) commented on the presence of a Spanish genetic marker in the Shackleford herd:

> It can be difficult to determine whether there is direct Spanish ancestry in a lot of the wild populations, because breeds like the Narragansett Pacer were important in the development of

. . . as well as the Pryor Mountain horses. The herds live live on opposite sides of the continent, but closely resemble each other. Both herds trace back to Spanish horses—probably those bred on the islands of the Caribbean to supply Spanish explorers and colonists. Additionally, certain individuals in both herds carry the rare Q-ac genetic marker denoting old Spanish bloodlines.

> some of the North American breeds. . . . in a feral herd, you don't know whether the marker is from old Spanish bloodlines, or is from these North American breeds which have some Spanish heritage.

There is variation within any breed, and even the original Jennets showed differences in conformation and attributes. Sponenberg and Reed (2009) developed a 5-point matrix that scores traits related to Colonial Spanish type. Horses are graded from 1 to 5 on specific physical attributes. The examiner scores each feature of the horse, adds the results, and then divides the total by the number of items. A score of 1 indicates strongly Iberian conformation, 2 is acceptable, and 3 is marginal. Ratings of 4 and 5 indicate significantly non-Spanish features. In a purely Spanish herd, scores should cluster around 1 and 2, with very few in 4 and none in 5.

An individual horse of a non-Spanish breed may have a low score, but when more than 80% of horses in a given population have low scores on this scale, the herd is likely to be Iberian in origin. Herds with 50% or fewer Iberian types either do not have Spanish heritage, or interbreeding with unrelated breeds has diluted the gene pool until Iberian genes are no longer widely expressed.

As a species, all horses have five or six lumbar vertebrae or show a partial fusion of the fifth and sixth. Many or most Colonial Spanish horses (but not all) have five lumbar vertebrae, but so do many other breeds. This trait is very common in Arabians and regularly occurs in other breeds as well, such as Thoroughbreds. Indeed, the Colonial Spanish Horse possibly owes his vertebrae count to the ancient proto-Arabians in his lineage.

Just because a horse has Colonial Spanish characteristics does not mean it can be considered part of the breed. Sponenberg (2011) writes that the frame overo pattern (a base of a solid color like black, bay, or chestnut splashed with irregular white patches which rarely extend to the back, lower legs, and tail) "is almost entirely limited to North American Colonial Spanish horses or their descendants." The author's registered Paint Horse, Chics War Eagle (Leonardo), demonstrates the frame overo pattern. His forebears include paints, Thoroughbreds, Quarter Horses, and, apparently, Spanish ancestors that bestowed his flashy coloration. Leonardo's pedigree traces to many of the horses mentioned in this book—Snip, Janus, Bulle Rock, the Godolphin Arabian, the Darley Arabian, the Byerley Turk. These great foundation horses are also prominent in the pedigrees of Morgans, American Saddlebreds, Tennessee Walking Horses, Standardbreds, Quarter Horses, and Thoroughbreds. The gene pool was smaller in colonial days, and wealthy breeders drew heavily on the services of a handful of elite stallions, resulting in kinship among outwardly diverse American breeds.

Virtually all the Corolla and Shackleford horses are sorrel, chestnut, bay, brown, or black. The graying gene was once present in the Corolla herd, but it is unknowable whether this color was native or introduced. The Shackleford herd contained duns, buckskins, and palominos before 1996, when North Carolina health officials euthanized 74 horses that tested positive for equine infectious anemia. A few Corollas exhibit the white ticking of the rabicano trait, and at least two have spashy white sabino spots on their bellies. Many of the Carrot Island horses are line back red duns, and the Cedar Island herd has two buckskin mares, mother and daughter. All are small horses, mostly 12–14 hands (48–56 in./1.22–1.42 m), with Colonial Spanish conformation.

Historical photographs and written accounts of Banker Horses describe them much as they are today in color, size, and conformation. The modern herd at the Ocracoke Pony Pen, however, shows evidence of crossbreeding. The Ocracoke herd has two dominant colors not found in any other Banker herds, tobiano pinto and gray. As a dominant trait, tobiano is expressed in nearly every generation, sometimes so minimally that the white markings may go unnoticed. Gray is also a dominant trait—every gray horse has at least one gray parent. When grays or tobianos suddenly appear in a herd of horses where they have been historically absent, the trait has been brought in by an outside horse. It appears that gray and tobiano both appeared in the herd in the 20th century. Dunbar, (1958) gave evidence of this crossbreeding when he wrote that the Ocracoke ponies had been "recently improved and should not be considered Banks ponies or Tackies."

Two gray stallions are known to have been introduced to Ocracoke. Phillip Howard, a native Ocracoker, relates how his great-grandfather, James Howard, brought a two-year old gray Arabian stallion to the island "from somewhere on the mainland" in the 1880s (Howard, 2002). Jim Howard kept White Dandy in Ocracoke Village and may have bred him to Banker mares. Because White Dandy was an Arabian, any foals sired by him would be half-Arabian crossbreds. In the 1980s, Cape Hatteras National Seashore used the services of a purebred gray Andalusian stallion named Cubanito "to breed with Banker mares to insure an adequate gene pool" (Henning, 1985, p. 3). Unfortunately, the Andalusian breed is only distantly related to the Colonial Spanish horse, and Cubanito's introduction was essentially a crossbreeding that undermined the genetic integrity of the herd. Before horses were brought in from Shackleford Banks and Corolla to increase genetic variability, the average horse in the Ocracoke herd was about 15 hands (60 in./1.5 m), considerably larger than a Colonial Spanish Horse.

So what exactly are Banker Horses? We know that they descended from Spanish lineage, probably through the Chickasaw Horses brought from the West by Indian traders, Seminole Horses brought north from Florida, and Spanish horses from the West Indies introduced by British colonists. It is possible that the Narragansett Pacer, the Galloway, the Irish Hobby, and other light European saddle horses contributed their genes to the Banks herds centuries ago, and there is some evidence that Quarter Horses were added to the Pea Island herd more recently.

If outside genes were added episodically to "improve" the bloodlines, a common practice among stockmen, these contributions would likely have come from breeds or types already found in, or frequently imported to the Carolinas. Outcrosses appear to have been infrequent, however. Although there is no way to know for sure, it appears that these horses have bred primarily with one another, or with horses of similar breeding introduced from the mainland since the late 1600s or even earlier, and have developed into a unique and rare strain of Colonial Spanish Horse. The Carolina Banker Horse represents a critically endangered strain of perhaps the oldest surviving American horse breed. Conant et al., writing about the Colonial Spanish horses of the Southeast, commented that "these relic populations are worth preserving, both for their genetic as well as their historical heritage as descendants of the first modern horses in the Americas" (2012, p. 62). In 2010, North Carolina designated the Colonial Spanish Mustang as the official state horse.

Shipwrecks were commonplace on the hazardous shoals of the Carolina coast, many of them were undocumented. It is possible that horses swimming from wrecked ships might have originated or augmented the North Carolina barrier island herds. Any horses reaching shore from a shipwreck would most likely have been bred in the New World. Before the mid-1700s, they would have been Spanish horses from the West Indies (or, less often, European horses) bound for the Eastern Seaboard. Thereafter, any shipwrecked horses would have most likely originated in New England or another British colony on the North American mainland.

To warn ships of dangerous shoals, the Ocracoke Lighthouse was constructed in 1823. The white brick structure remains one of the oldest functioning navigational aids in the United States. Confederates extinguished the light in 1861, and Union forces resurrected it in 1864. After 1874, the federal government sought to improve marine safety by extending coverage by the U.S. Lifesaving Service to the Outer Banks. Based at stations positioned various distances apart along the coast, its men monitored the beaches and struggled to

Ocracoke's patriarch stallion, Santiago, is a brilliantly marked black and white tobiano. Some members of the Ocracoke herd carry two dominant genes not found in any of the other Banker herds, for tobiano pinto and gray coloration. Because these colors appeared suddenly in the 20th century, their presence can be attributed to outcrossing.

rescue sailors from stormy seas. Where he could, a surfman walked half the distance to the next station, scanning as he went; turned a key in a clock or exchanged a token with another surfman; then walked back, no matter whether nature offered raw, biting winds, blazing heat, or hurricane. The more horrendous the storm, the more likely their services would be needed.

Unflappable, loyal, sensible Banker Horses worked in partnership with the men of the Lifesaving Service. In the very early days, the Lifesaving Service expected its men to patrol the beach on foot and to push or pull the surfboats and beach apparatus carts unaided. Each of those burdens weighed half a ton/450 kg or more, and the stations were miles apart, so the crews had a strong incentive to provide their own mounts and draft animals at no cost to the government. When the service officially authorized horses and their accommodations, keepers or district inspectors may have bought horses from local stockmen. The tireless horses hauled equipment over the sand to shipwreck sites and often entered surging surf in the most violent tempests as their riders rescued people from the waves. In one famous act of heroism, Rasmus Midgett, a 48-year-old surfman from the Gull Shoal Station patrolling the beach around 3 a.m. at the height of the Category 3 San Ciriaco Hurricane of 1899, pulled 10 men from the wreck of the barkentine *Priscilla* aided only by his Banker horse Tom Creef (Henning, 1985).

One reason Portsmouth was established and a fort was built nearby was to protect the area against attacks by Spanish pirates and privateers in the mid-18th century. Throughout the 1740s, Spanish privateers attacked ships off the Outer Banks. (In the spring of 1741, two Spanish ships captured six vessels in 10 days.) They established camp in Ocracoke, burned houses, and killed cattle. In 1747, they briefly seized Beaufort. The next year, they sacked the town of Brunswick, on the lower Cape Fear River, which never recovered.

The short, mostly fictional golden age of piracy on the Outer Banks occurred a few decades earlier, between 1713 and 1718, when brigands such as Christopher Moody, John Cole, Robert Deal, Charles Vane, Richard Worley, "Calico Jack" Rackham, Stede Bonnet, and Edward Teach, the infamous Blackbeard, terrorized—and occasionally visited—the area. They ranged all over the western Atlantic, but sometimes used the barrier islands as hideouts and

A band of Bankers climbs Penny (Lewark) Hill on Currituck Banks. Over the centuries Banker horses have developed unique hooves adapted for running in sand. This band shows the two most typical hoof shapes: the sorrels have wide hooves that spread the horse's weight over a wider surface area and prevent sinking. The black has hooves with a strong, steep wall and a deeply cupped sole that let them sink in and provide traction. These unique hoof shapes are present at birth.

preyed on cargo-laden ships around Ocracoke Inlet and the Cape Hatteras bottleneck.

Blackbeard, probably an Englishman who served as a privateer during Queen Anne's War, turned to piracy in 1716, and by 1718 he employed about 400 men on four ships. He commandeered a 14-gun French slave ship, the *Concorde*, and made her his flagship, increasing her armament to 40 guns and renaming her *Queen Anne's Revenge*.

Blackbeard arrived in North Carolina in June 1718, sought and received a royal pardon from Governor Charles Eden (who apparently benefitted from the buccaneer's spoils), and settled in the colony's capital, Bath, where Eden lived. His presence there, as well as his alliances with other lawbreakers, created a state of alarm among regional maritime interests. When Eden ignored their concerns, frustrated Ocracokers and other coastal residents sought help from Governor Alexander Spotswood of Virginia. Spotswood seized the opportunity to eliminate a criminal while embarrassing a corrupt colleague.

Governor Spotswood hired two light, fast sloops that arrived off North Carolina's Outer Banks on November 21. It was Lieutenant Robert Maynard, aboard the *Ranger*, that killed Blackbeard on November 22, 1718, in a furious battle at Ocracoke Inlet. The pirate allegedly received five musket-ball wounds and more than 20 sword lacerations before he succumbed. In only two years of pirating, Blackbeard had taken more than 50 ships. Maynard sailed up the Pamlico River to Bath with Blackbeard's severed head swinging from his bowsprit. On November 21, 1996, a wreck that may be *Queen Anne's Revenge* was discovered by the private firm Intersal near Beaufort Inlet under 20 ft/6 m of water.

Some believe that the wild horses originated with pirates who brought them to Ocracoke as a source of mounts or even food if necessary, but scholars discredit this idea. Though pirates probably did kill and eat free-roaming livestock, the herds were evidently well established before pirates arrived. Contrary to popular lore, most pirates were not native to the Banks, and the local population had little involvement with piracy.

Pirates were not the only ones who dined on meat stolen from the barrier islands. Stock was abundant and largely unguarded. Mariners of all ethnicities frequently availed themselves of this source of sustenance. British forces took hundreds of cattle and sheep from Ocracoke and Portsmouth during the War of 1812 alone.

The islanders developed a unique dialect with turns of speech distinct from those of mainland North Carolinians. On Ocracoke, *high tide* is pronounced \häi 'täid\, usually, inaccurately rendered *hoi toide*. A dragonfly is a *skeeter hawk*. The term *abreast* is used as a preposition to mean "across from," as in "'He lives up here abreast the post office' and 'She went aground abreast the island'" (Howren, 1962, p. 174). A grove of trees is a *hammock* \'həm•ək\. A single cow or bull is a *cattle-beast*. *Airish* means breezy. *Begombed* is soiled, as in "Your shirt's begombed with grease." To *mommuck* is to damage or destroy. Edible shore birds such as curlews and sandpipers are *sea chickens* (Impact Assessment, 2005, vol. 2, pp. 509–511).

Visitors arrived by mail boat, which could carry up to 35 passengers and freight in addition to letters and packages. Around 1915, there were "sailing vessels (sharpies) with auxiliary motors" (Goerch, 1995/1995, p. 55) that left Washington, N.C., Wednesdays

Edward Teach, a.k.a. Blackbeard, often intimidated victims into submission with his wild appearance and reputation for ruthlessness. He frequently wore his long, black beard in beribboned braids and stuck burning cannon fuses under his hat brim. In his two years of piracy, he and his men took more than 50 ships.

and Saturdays at 8 p.m. for the overnight trip to Ocracoke. The Taylor Brothers started a daily ferry service between Atlantic and Ocracoke in the spring of 1960. In 1963, the state took over the ferry and shifted operations to Cedar Island.

Every family on Ocracoke had at least one horse, and each of the free-roaming horses had a nominal owner. But many, if not most, of Ocracoke's horses lived their lives, birth to death, running wild, breeding at will, deliberately handled by human beings only during pony pennings.

Living wild sometimes posed dangers to the horses. Sometimes one would get stuck in a marsh until his herdmates rescued him by pushing him out. During one storm, a band gathered at the tip of a peninsula. Floods cut off their escape, and every one drowned.

A Park Service ethnohistorical research project describes the life of a typical Outer Banker. Before the advent of cars and buses, islanders traveled across land via horse and cart. A villager described "flat carts" that allowed one to sit on the edge with "your feet dangled down between the shaft and the horse," that is, along the front edge of the cart where the horse's harness attached. Bankers also rode horses bareback after catching them on the beach. A villager recalled when she and her brother were sent after one of her father's mares. They approached "Mary" with bridle in hand, but the mare was in heat and a stallion challenged the children:

> We were both going to ride her bareback. But here come this old stallion. He'd rare up on his hind legs and scream. Honey, that was two scared kids. You talking about somebody praying. We'd get on one side and when he'd come at us, we'd go on the opposite side. We kept inching along until he ran back to his brood. We'd be a-crying telling Dad about it. He said, "Well, next time I'll give you a gig and gig him like that. And, very calmly, mother said, "No, Jim, there won't be a next time."
> (Impact Assessment, 2005, vol. 1, pp. 243–244)

According to one account, boys of Hatteras Village in the 1920s spent much of their free time

> chasing horses on the beach and breaking them. It was easy to break a two-year old in the soft sand; "he'd settle right down and get easy." Horses were typically caught on "Friday or Saturday mornings," ridden on the weekends and "turned loose Mondays—let them graze on the beach the rest of the week."
> (Impact Assessment, 2005, vol. 2, p. 307)

In 1920, federal agents built concrete dipping vats along the Outer Banks in an effort to eradicate tick-borne disease. The U.S. Department of Agriculture required stockmen to round up free-roaming cattle and herd them through a toxic "creosote mixture" (Impact

Hitched to the porch rail, horses wait patiently for their riders to return. Photograph courtesy of the Ocracoke Preservation Society.

Assessment, 2005, vol. 1, p. 214) every other week. Many of the solutions used contained compounds of toxic, carcinogenic arsenic. Stockmen marked the rump of each dipped animal with a splash of green paint and searched for unmarked animals. A local described the dipping process:

> They drug them through that dipping vat. They'd swim through [a formula] like Lysol mixed in five-gallon jugs. . . .
>
> And DDT—they'd empty the solution, pull the plug and it would run right out in the sand. So you know it got in the water. That could be the reason the cancer rate is so high. Probably a dozen in Avon right now with it. And that's a lot

for a small village like that. (Impact Assessment, 2005, vol. 1, pp. 214–215)

Teenaged boys were happy to participate. Said one resident, "We boys would get a kick out of being cowboys, rounding up the cattle and horses and driving them through this dipping vat" (Impact Assessment, 2005, vol. 2, p. 307).

Apparently many other Bankers resisted the stock-dipping mandate. Lee (2008, pp. 104–105) writes,

Islanders responded first by dynamiting the concrete vats, only to repair them, apparently under threat of prosecution. When agents came to oversee dips in the first years of the program, villagers passively resisted by refusing to participate. After finally compelling villagers to contribute to the federal effort, many of the animals proved too feral to be corralled into pens . . . the county offered villagers five dollars a head to shoot any cattle that could not be dipped, and locals eliminated about two-thirds of the nearly 400 cattle in Dare County before the USDA declared the area tick-free after the 1924 season.

At Cape Hatteras, men gathered free-roaming horses and cattle twice yearly for identification and sale. One elderly resident remembered "'When I was young, there was cattle and horses just roaming around everywhere, like the old west. . . . The old guys used to round the cattle up all the way from Avon. They would bring them to the pound to mark the cows and brand the colts'" (Impact Assessment, 2005, vol. 1, p. 150). Leland Tillett (b. 1913) recalled cattle drives from Oregon Inlet to the Virginia line, and Ermie Bowden (b. 1925) recalled that there were more than 3,000 cattle just from False Cape to Carova. Chater (1926) estimated that there were 5,000–6,000 horses on the Banks. A decade later, all the free-roaming livestock had been removed from the Banks except for small populations on Ocracoke, Currituck Banks, and Shackleford Banks. The last semi-feral cow was shot in 1938.

On Ocracoke, the July 4th pony penning was a long-anticipated celebration, a festival of hard work and hard play. Each Ocracoke family had its own brand, and foals were matched to mothers and emblazoned with an owner's logo. Banker Horses were in demand on the mainland and many were sold off the island during these roundups.

Wild ponies follow the Ocracoke shoreline in the 1950s. Note the low dunes and the grasses cropped short by grazing. Photograph courtesy of Ocracoke Preservation Society.

Once off the island they had to adapt to confinement and transition from a diet of marsh grass to one of hay and grain, but most were domesticated with relative ease.

Traditionally, the roundup began on July 3, when a handful of Ocracoke's cowboys would ride north, to the periphery of the wild herds that grazed in places with such fanciful names as Tar Hole Plains. The horsemen would camp overnight near the sound, and in the morning the roundup would begin. They rode in McClellan saddles, a style devised by General George McClellan, adopted by the U.S. Army in 1859, and used in the Civil War.

Captain James W. Howard, who ran the Hatteras Inlet Lifesaving Station for many years, bought a dapple-gray 2-year-old Arabian colt from the mainland in the late 1800s. An 1888 photograph shows 49-year-old Howard astride the high-headed mount, named "White Dandy" by his son Homer. Young Homer took to riding White Dandy, and was and White Dandy were renowned for his ability to round up more than 200 wild ponies without assistance.

Homer's son Marvin wrote,

> On "White Dandy" Homer on many occasions started at the north end of the island in the cool of the morning, driving the herd of wild ponies south. He rode merrily along across Tar-Ho[l]e Plains. There he would come upon a second herd of ponies headed by "Old Wildy," a long, rangy stallion. This herd, too, he would start driving southward. The third herd

he encountered at Scraggly Cedars, then the Great Swash. After passing Great Swash he came to Knoll Cedars where the sheep pen used to be, and from there on southward the driving got touchy and more strenuous for the herds from the north were reluctant to go farther south and would try to cut through the thickets or sand hills back northward.

There were about two-hundred wild ponies in those days. They had to be driven over sand hills, through bogs, across creeks, through marshes, and through woodland thickets of myrtle, cedar, oak and yaupon. At about ten o'clock in the morning of pony-penning day, the horses could be seen spread out on the plains around "First Hammock Hills," just north of Ocracoke Village. Each little band was headed by a tough and stringy stallion. They ran hither and thither, their manes and tails flying, heads held high, ears pointed forward, and necks arched to meet a foe. And whenever the stallions met, they did battle—biting, kicking, pawing—until the rider closed in. Then, they veered off from each other, returning to their herds. It was no easy task to drive these wild ponies sixteen miles [sic] southward to the corral in Ocracoke Village. (Howard, 1976, p. 26)

Horse Pen Point was the destination for many years, though other locations were favored throughout the 20th century.

"Interest in the once-wild Banker Ponies is a long tradition in the Howard family," says Philip Howard (2002), grandson of Homer, son of Lawton, and nephew of Marvin.

My father often told me about the time in 1926 when he was 15 years old. It was July and the annual Independence Day pony penning was in jeopardy of not happening because several of the young men were squabbling about something and no one was prepared to round up the horses. My dad and his best friend, Ansley O'Neal, though still teenagers, decided that they were old enough to tackle this responsibility. They mounted their ponies on July 3 and rode all the way to Hatteras Inlet (this was long before there were any paved roads on the island) where they camped out under the stars. Early the next morning the two boys began chasing the first small herd southward, toward the village. As they encountered each

Ocracoke village *circa* 1950s. Courtesy of the Ocracoke Preservation Society.

succeeding herd they forced them to join the others. Occasionally some of the animals would swim out into Pamlico Sound and make the boys' job much more difficult. Finally, after a grueling day of hard riding in the blazing summertime sun Lawton and Ansley rode proudly into the village behind several hundred stampeding Outer Banks ponies. It was a proud day for them both, and a fond memory for my father until the day he died.

Sometimes the cowboys would break the horses "Wild West style" before shipping them to the mainland. The designated animal was moved into an individual pen and crowded against the rail. The stockman grasped his tail through the fence, tied his head to a post, and placed a blindfold over his eyes before working a saddle onto his back. A cowboy would mount to take the ride. Off came the blindfold, and the horse was released. The frantic pony would run, buck, pivot, twist, rear, and sunfish, but the tenacious cowboy usually stuck to the horse's back like a leech. At last the pony would acquiesce, sweating and blowing, and let the rider direct him around the pen.

Homer Howard was skilled in breaking the willful, powerful wild stallions:

To catch a wild stallion with nothing but bare hands took wit, agility, strength, and stamina. Homer would walk quietly through the mares, slapping them on the rump, working his way between them slowly, gradually—getting closer and closer to a great stallion—crouching panther-like, ready, alert—and in a flash he was astride the stallion, holding its mane with his left hand, throwing his elbow over the horse's withers, hooking his knee behind the elbow of the horse's front leg, reaching out with his right hand to catch the horse's lower face just above the nostrils, clamping down tight, and sticking there with the tenacity of a bulldog. The stallion would rear, pitch, squeal, snort, paw the air for thirty of forty minutes, but finally, out of wind, tired, and afraid, he stopped his violent struggling. Slowly the horseman eased his grip; immediately, the stallion lunged and reared. Only after several attempts did the horse admit his defeat. "Old Widdie," "Guthrie Sam," and "Rainbow" and others were truly great stallions and had the spunk and grit to put up terrible battles. Their tusks, or cutting teeth, were long from age and could be used to cut and slash, and their forefeet and rear hoofs held a wicked kick. (Howard, 1976, p. 26).

Other horsemen trained Banker Horses with kindness, rewarding them with sweets, petting, and scratching of the itchy spots. Sometimes the first mounting was accomplished in the sound, with the horse belly-deep in water. This way, the horse's movements were restricted, and a thrown rider would have a soft landing. Horses gentled before riding usually put up no resistance.

Shipping the horses off Ocracoke presented a challenge. Ocracoke is 30 mi/48 km from the mainland, and ponies leaving the island were transported on flat barges, freight boats, or fishing boats. In one incident, two horses broke into the engine room of a fishing boat when a storm panicked them. Occasionally horses fell overboard and drowned.

Most Ocracoke natives enjoyed the pesky ponies. Hatteras Island had more villages, and people were less tolerant of livestock making themselves at home in their yards. Ocracoke Island had but one human settlement, at the south end, and Ocracokers comfortably shared their village with the animals.

The ponies wandered into town looking for handouts and would devour vegetable gardens if the gates were left open. One apparently developed a taste for fried fish and would reach his head into open windows to devour the family supper. Occasionally a family would be awakened long before dawn by an odd noise only to find an itchy pony scratching himself on the corner of the house. Occasionally a herd would stampede through town. They were small, beautiful animals with long, flowing manes and tails, tractable temperaments, and smooth gaits. The Ocracokers used them to pull carts and for plowing and rode them under saddle or bareback. Overall, the villagers and the horses coexisted in a relationship of mutual toleration and positive regard.

Over the years, horses from the mainland were introduced to improve the island stock. In the early 1900s, locals thought that the fleet, maneuverable Banker Horses would make superior polo ponies if only they were taller. In 1925, the stallion Beeswax was imported to Ocracoke Island for stud. Beeswax was the son of the champion polo pony Christopher Columbus, an English Thoroughbred imported to sire polo ponies and cavalry mounts. Beeswax was not rugged enough to withstand the rigors of life in the wild and was kept confined on a diet of hay and grain. His foals were popular, and most were sold to mainlanders for riding and polo. Elisha Ballance recalled, "'Back in the '20s, I believe, [David] Keppel brought a stud here, and he looked like and I think he was a Thoroughbred. He was a fine horse and couldn't live like the Bankers, had to be kept up and fed'" (Henning, 1985, p. 8). Henning maintains that the blood of Beeswax has been lost to Ocracoke over time, and none of his Thoroughbred genes remain in today's Banker herd.

Ballance also remembered large herds fortified by the introduction of Banker bloodlines from Hatteras Island, probably following the 1935 prohibition against free-roaming livestock. "There were plenty of horses up until the time I went into the Coast Guard in 1938," he said. "Some had been brought from Hatteras and turned out with the ones here, but they were Bankers, too, they got along" (Henning, 1985, p. 8). O'Neal et al. (1976, p. 24) describe a smaller herd: "As late as 1939 there were fifty to one-hundred ponies on Ocracoke, half of them continuing to run wild along the Banks, the other half broken in for riding by the island boys." They went on to say that there were no annual public roundups during the War years of the 1940s, and the "spectacular Fourth-of-July events have never been revived" (1976, p. 25).

Roaming horses were eradicated from Dare County, to the north, beginning in 1935 and forbidden in Currituck County in 1937, though never completely removed. Only the barrier chain between Hatteras Inlet and Beaufort Inlet—Ocracoke, Core Banks, and Shackleford Banks—retained wild herds.

A 1940 news article related,

> When soil conservation forces of the federal government four years ago began their most ambitious endeavor to check sand erosion along the Carolina banks, they soon realized that the banker ponies were rapidly eating the tough beach grasses and shrubs which they were carefully planting in long miles of brush panel fences to hold back the ocean.
>
> The suggestion that the banker ponies ought to be exterminated, in the interest of anchoring the shifting sand dunes, brought forth so many objections from the animals' friends that the proposal was abandoned. But more care was taken to keep the ponies away from the grass fences.
>
> Today there are said to be more ponies along the banks than there were a decade ago; but they still fall far short of the many thousands that roamed the sands years ago. ("Vegetation Scarcity Blamed on N.C. Oceanside Ponies," 1940, p. 10)

The horsemen suspended public roundups during the war years, and afterwards, the pony pennings were never as big or exciting. The number of ponies on the island was declining rapidly as well, from 200–300 in the 1800s to 70 in 1956 to 35 in 1957 by order of the Park Service to an all-time low of nine in 1976.

Marvin Howard retired from his military career to his home on Ocracoke Island and organized the world's only mounted Boy Scout troop. Howard, who found great satisfaction in working with both children and horses, founded Troop 290 in 1954, and most of the boys on the island enthusiastically joined. For the next 5 years, Howard served as scoutmaster to a total of 25 boys and advised them on the care and training of their mounts.

Barrier island horses can swim from their first day of life and frequently use water to escape from biting insects or the oppressive heat of summer. These Ocracoke horses were apparently undisturbed by the activities of working boats in Silver Lake around 1957. Photograph by Hugh Morton, from the Hugh Morton Collection of Photographs and Films #P0081, © North Carolina Collection, University of North Carolina at Chapel Hill Library.

For the barefoot boys of Ocracoke, the Scout troop and the ponies were the focus of their lives. Each boy began by selecting a wild pony to catch, train, and ride. Each pony, though living free, had an owner. Some were privately owned, and some were legally the property of the Park Service, which had acquired most of the island for inclusion in Cape Hatteras National Seashore. The price was $50 per pony, a steep sum for a young boy on a poor, remote island in the 1950s and equivalent to more than $400 today . To earn money, the boys spent countless afternoons mowing lawns and helping fishermen with the day's catch.

The boys knew each of the wild horses well, and after much observation, deliberation, and daydreaming, they would set their sights on particular horses, often fractious young stallions. Usually two boys set out after the chosen pony, which had no desire to be captured. The wild bands evaded the boys at every turn, often venturing out into the marshes or the water to escape. Because castrating a colt makes him more tractable, most male horses are gelded young, but the Scouts largely preferred to ride stallions.

Riding shoulder to shoulder and in groups, the boys galloped bareback down the beach on stallions that had been rivals in the wild. The feisty ponies were used to having their own way and often resisted domestication, especially at first. One time, so the tale goes, a rowdy stallion aptly named "Little Teach" bucked a Scout from his back, kicking him in the head for emphasis. A vacationing doctor, slightly inebriated, successfully sewed up the scalp wound with 44 stitches.

The Scouts followed many time-honored Ocracoke techniques of horse breaking, including mounting blindfolded horses as they stood belly-deep in the sound. They experimented with filling an old pair of pants with sand and tying it around the pony so that he could expend his bucking energy on an inanimate object rather than a Scout. Unfortunately, the ponies usually dislodged the pants and trampled them. The Scouts realized that it was best not to reinforce the trampling of what they bucked off in case one of them might be the next victim.

Howard coached the boys in training methods and horsemanship, and they met most of their Scouting requirements on horseback. The boys also had the opportunity to show off their skills at the Pirates' Jamboree, a celebration that featured races and other tests of riding ability. Annually the troop would compete in the horse races held on the beach at Hatteras and at Buxton, which was no small undertaking.

The boys would set out early and ride a total of 26 mi/42 km to reach Buxton. To cross Hatteras Inlet, a dozen boys would lead their blindfolded ponies onto the little ferry and hold them on the open deck of the rocking, groaning boat for the 40-min crossing, a situation that would have panicked other horses. The boys then rode from Hatteras to Buxton, about 12 mi/19 km. After arriving at Buxton, the boys would race in four quarter-mile (400-m) heats, often besting stiff competition that included Arabians and Quarter Horses.

Five hundred to 600 cattle still roamed Ocracoke Island during this period, and the Scouts became skilled at sorting and penning them for branding. The fee for filing a brand with the County Register of Deeds was the same as it had been for many years—$0.10. At the July

In the 1950s, Ocracoke was home to the only mounted Boy Scout troop. Marvin Howard is mounted at the far right. Photograph courtesy of the Ocracoke Preservation Society.

4th pony penning celebrations, they displayed their superb horsemanship skills for the benefit of the visitors.

The Ocracoke mounted Scouts captured national attention when they were featured in *Boy's Life* magazine (Brooks, 1956) and in a children's novel, *Wild Pony Island* (Meader, 1959). The Scouts also helped around town and served as mounted honor guards for the Coast Guard. During the summer, the boys helped keep Ocracoke's mosquitoes at bay by spraying the marshes with insecticide. Astride sure-footed marsh ponies, they were able to penetrate the wide flats of muck far more easily than anyone else.

The sturdy Banker Ponies cost virtually nothing to maintain. The Scouts could choose to let the horses run free to be captured when needed, because they remained sleek and well-fleshed on a diet of marsh grass. Most of the boys, however, opted to build stalls in their back yards to keep their horses close at hand. Unlike wild ponies, a penned Banker Pony does not have the luxury of grazing 17 hr a day on dense wild grasses. As the ponies got less grazing and more exercise, they needed a dietary supplement such as grain, a concentrated

Pony Penning, July 4, 1956, at the Sam Jones Corral. Although Ocracoke supported hundreds of wild horses though the 18th and 19th centuries, the census fell sharply after World War II and dwindled further with the arrival of the National Park Service. In 1956 there were only about 70 free-roaming horses on the island. The following year, the Park Service had eliminated all but the 35 owned by the Boy Scouts and helped them build a pen to confine them. This photograph may show the last Pony Penning on Ocracoke. Photograph by Aycock Brown, courtesy of Outer Banks History Center.

energy source. When the boys offered sweet feed, a tasty grain-and-molasses mixture that most horses relish, the ponies did not know what to do with it. The Scouts initially had to place it in their mouths until they noticed the sweet flavor and realized that it was food. It was not long before they discovered the pleasure of other flavors as well. Many Scout ponies developed a taste for soda pop.

The horses often formed close bonds with their owners and when released to run free would often visit them in the village when they wanted human companionship. Some ponies would come running at the sound of their owner's whistle.

When Cape Hatteras NS took over Ocracoke Island, it was a mixed blessing. The new status would offer some protection against the hotels, cottages, restaurants, miniature golf courses, and tourist attractions that had overtaken many East Coast beaches. But the

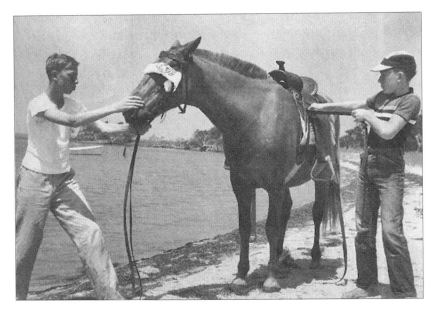

The Ocracoke Scouts would select a pony, often a stallion, from the wild herds and pay its nominal owner the price of purchase. Working together, they trained the horses to accept saddles and bridles. Photograph courtesy of the Ocracoke Preservation Society.

Park Service did not recognize free-roaming horses as repatriated wildlife and did not want them competing with the native wildlife that it was charged to protect. It removed the cattle, pigs, sheep, and goats that roamed the island by the late 1950s and saw no reason to treat horses any differently.

Ocracokers loved their horses, however. To them, the free-roaming ponies were an important element of the island's character. Lawmakers and regulators argued that not enough was known about the horses' past to support claims that they had historical value. There were high emotions on both sides of the argument.

Marvin Howard, whose family had been involved with the Banker Ponies since the 1700s, worked relentlessly to save the Ocracoke herd. During the late 1950s, at least eight ponies died of Eastern equine encephalitis, a mosquito-borne viral illness. Rudy Austin, an original Scout, lost his two mounts, Diabolo and Blaze, to the disease.

When Highway 12 was opened on Ocracoke in 1957, the posted speed limit of 50 mph/80 kph posed a new danger to the horses. The

Scouts petitioned to fence a large pasture for the horses as a sort of a compromise—the horses would not roam entirely free anymore, but they would remain on the island to be enjoyed as a reminder of Ocracoke's bygone days.

The North Carolina General Assembly finally, but confusingly, ended free range on parts of the Outer Banks not already under the stock law. N.C. General Statute 68-42, which took effect July 1, 1958, made two exceptions: "horses known as marsh ponies or banks ponies" on Ocracoke Island and Shackleford Banks. The next year, the General Assembly directed the Sheriff of Carteret County to kill or remove all other livestock from Core and Shackleford Banks (An Act To Provide for the Removal of Cattle Remaining on Core Banks, 1959), which the state Supreme Court upheld in *Chadwick v. Salter* (1961). The exception to these exceptions was a group of up to 35 horses owned by the Scout troop, which the law implicitly required to be fenced. But G.S. 68-43 made the Scouts' horses subject to removal by the state no matter whether they were fenced. By this time, however, the Park Service owned most of Ocracoke, and as a federal agency it was not bound by state law to let horses live on its property within or without fences.

The Park Service eventually granted the Scouts a special-use permit and provided fence posts. Residents raised money for fencing and for the first year of supplemental feeding. The state of North Carolina also contributed funds toward the new lifestyle of the ponies for the first year. The animals were finally penned in 1959. It was a fairly easy task to put the herd within fences, but keeping them contained proved challenging. When the ponies wearied of confinement, they simply knocked over the posts and broke the wire. The Scouts would leave school to recover the ponies and mend fences. The Scouts enjoyed this task—so much, in fact, that they would often sneak back to the pasture after dark and push over posts, ensuring another holiday from school.

In the mid-1960s, the Boy Scouts of America ruled that if the Ocracokers were to maintain a mounted troop, its members would have to carry insurance. The boys could not afford insurance, and Ocracoke's mounted Scout troop dismounted after only about 10 years.

The Park Service took over management of the ponies in the late 1960s, when the herd was on the verge of extinction. In 1973, Park

The rebellious element of Ocracoke Island: teenagers riding bareback on fast horses, cigarettes in hand. Even though the Scouts weren't immune to the usual vices, Howard often mentioned the lack of juvenile delinquency on Ocracoke, which he saw as a direct result of involvement with the ponies. Photograph courtesy of the Ocracoke Preservation Society.

Ranger Jim Henning was transferred to Ocracoke from Bodie Island. He took an interest in the herd stallion, also named Jim. With his wife, Jeannetta, Henning wholeheartedly devoted himself to the resurrection of the herd.

When the Hennings first arrived, the ponies were malnourished, wormy, and in dire need of veterinary care. Dr. Jasper Needham, a veterinarian on Hatteras Island, came in to vaccinate the animals, trim hooves to resolve gait abnormalities, and deworm the animals.

Internal parasites are more of a problem for domestic horses than for their wild counterparts. Locals say that the marsh grass diet serves as a natural dewormer and is effective also for cattle. More likely, wild horses have fewer parasites because they range over a larger area than their domesticated relatives and avoid areas contaminated by manure. Penned horses feed in areas where others defecate and are likely to pick up worm eggs while grazing. By this time the Ocracoke herd had been confined to a 180-acre pen and exchanging parasites for 14 years.

Chutes and pens made veterinary care less of a rodeo event. Before they were built, dewormer medication was given in a large trough mixed with food. The horses would compete over the offering. Often the dominant animals received too much, subordinates not enough. Using a chute, caretakers could administer dewormer in precise doses via oral syringe.

By the 1970s, fertility decreased until there were no births in one 5-year span. The last remaining Ocracoke stallion was genetically incompatible with three of his mares. These mares could deliver healthy foals, but antibodies in their colostrum, or first milk, would attack and destroy the newborns' red blood cells, a condition called neonatal isoerythrolysis. At the time this condition was attributed to excessive inbreeding, but this assumption was later proved false. Blood-type incompatibility is less likely in an inbred population because closely related horses tend to have the same blood types.

The Hennings rescued three foals by bottle-feeding them, but something more had to be done. To save the herd from extinction, the Park Service brought in an Andalusian stallion named Cubanito in the 1980s. Modern Andalusians exhibit Spanish characteristics similar to those of the ancient Jennet. Cubanito was a handsome example of the breed.

Although bringing in outside blood resulted in live foals, Cubanito has since been criticized as a choice for this role. As it turns out, Cubanito carried both of the genes necessary to perpetuate neonatal isoerythrolysis. When he was bred to the three problem mares, however, the resulting offspring were healthy and robust. The herd was on the increase again, but was no longer true to the original bloodlines.

Andalusians, like Banker Horses, are of Spanish origin, but the modern Andalusian is not closely related to the modern Banker Horse. Conant et al. wrote (2011, p. 61), "North American Colonial Spanish Horses show more similarity to other New World horses of Iberian origin than they do to the modern Lusitano and Andalusian." The matings to Cubanito amounted to crossbreeding, moving the genes of the Ocracoke herd away from their original lines. Several

The Ocracoke Pony Pen confines the ponies to a tiny fraction of their historic habitat.

Ocracoke horses had been officially accepted by the Spanish Mustang registry, but Cubanito's foals were ineligible for registration.

The Park Service also tried to introduce a horse named Sailor, who was born on Ocracoke and removed to Hatteras by Dale Burrus when the Park Service was selling off the wild ponies. The mares wanted nothing to do with Sailor. He did manage to sire three or four foals, all males, but the mares never fully accepted him.

Compounding problems of genetic and emotional incompatibility, some of the mares simply stopped conceiving. Hormone therapy was initiated in 1977, and subsequently three of the four problem mares foaled.

In addition, the foals had a run of bad luck. One died at birth. Three died from overeating. One punctured his foot as a newborn, probably on a reed out in the marsh. A tendon contracted until he was walking on his fetlock rather than his hoof. He underwent surgery and was fitted with a cast, and he ultimately survived.

With veterinary care, the Ocracoke herd began to recover. One mare reached the astonishing age of 40, more than 100 in human years. In her last year she gave birth to a foal probably sired by Sailor. (Unlike a woman, whose reproductive capacity ends at about two thirds of her lifespan, a mare is never too old to conceive, though fertility decreases with age.) She was initially unable to rise after the birth, but she lived another 6 months, hand-fed by the Hennings.

In 1977, a pinto colt named Mr. Bobby or Mr. Bob was born to a spotted mare, "Old Paint," and the sorrel stallion Jim. Jim Henning broke him to saddle and put him to use in living history programs and parades. In 1981 Park Ranger Howard Bennink used him to patrol the beach and to manage crowds at festivals. Mr. Bob became the first horse in Ocracoke's National Park Service Beach Patrol. He died in the fall of 2010 at the age of 33.

In 2010, there were 21 horses in the Ocracoke herd. Some are larger than many Banker Ponies, apparently because of outcrossing to Cubanito and maybe other outside horses. Most stand between 14 and 15.2 hands at the withers (56–62 in/1.32–1.57 m) and weigh about 1,000 lb/450 kg each.

The Ocracoke pony pen remains a popular attraction. A boardwalk and viewing platform flank the front pastures, allowing even the least adventurous visitor an opportunity to watch the ponies. Park Service educational programs allow tourists and schoolchildren a closer look at these horses. Annual vacationers take pleasure in watching the foals mature into adults.

The Ocracoke horses live in domesticity, accustomed to the usual husbandry routines of feeding, watering, grooming, and mucking stalls. Horse people generally do not find these chores onerous, but approach the physical maintenance of their charges with the same pleasure a gardener finds in working with the earth. A number of volunteers assist with the chores inherent in maintaining the Ocracoke herd, and for them it is a labor of love and a passion.

While many people stop at the Pony Pen just long enough to snap a couple of photographs, others spend peaceful hours observing the ponies' behavior and watching them interact. Wild or domestic, horses communicate mostly through postures, gestures, and facial expressions that can be readily interpreted by human observers. Body language allows them to communicate and maintain social order without extraneous noises that could draw predators.

In the wild, the horse that belongs to a group is less likely to be targeted by predators and will more likely to survive to pass on his or her genes. Equine social behavior minimizes conflict and promotes group stability. The social order within a band is complex and

Face grizzled and muscles wasting, this horse is well into his 30s. The Ocracoke herd has a number of elderly horses and would soon die out if not for recent emphasis on preserving the strain.

stratified. Mares tend to form long-term social bonds with other mares. These friendships increase foal birth rates and foal survival, probably by reducing harassment by stallions.

Horses are attuned to subtle changes in the body language of their companions. There is meaning in the flick of an ear or the retraction of a nostril. Horses are able to recognize other horses from a distance by appearance and posture as well as by the scent of the body, hoofprints, or manure.

The outline of the horse's body is an important visual signal to herdmates. An excited, alert horse has a high-headed, high-tailed outline; a straight back and low head and tail signal relaxation. The alarm posture—head and tail raised, nostrils flared, eyes wide, usually accompanied by an inspiratory snort—alerts the herd to possible danger.

Many parts of the body can be used independently for signaling. Tails are particularly expressive. An excited horse may carry its tail lifted like a flag, particularly while running. Tail flagging is especially pronounced in Arabian horses. A tail clamped tightly against

Colonial Spanish Banker Horses in the Ocracoke Pony Pen in the 1990s displaying a variety of colors and sizes.

the rump indicates fear. Horses swish their tails when annoyed, and when the insects are biting, tails in constant motion serve as fly swatters. A mare will raise her tail and carry it to the side to display her vulva when in heat.

Horses have excellent hearing and can move their ears independently. They can turn their ears toward the focus of attention and flatten them to protect them from loud noises. Horses grazing in a group monitor human visitors by keeping one eye and one ear on the newcomers, usually without a pause in feeding. Ears are laid back to show aggression and flattened to the neck in battle to prevent them from being bitten off by a rival. Two ears directed sideways convey uncertainty or insecurity. Horses seem able to use body positioning to amplify sounds by bouncing them off their shoulders. Dogs and humans are better able to localize sound sources, but horses can hear higher-pitched sounds than humans and can hear a broader range of frequencies than most other animals.

Horses are capable of complex facial expressions and, like people, clearly show thoughts and emotions through their eyes. The white scleras of their eyes may show when the animal is anxious, but the eyes of many Appaloosa and pinto horses show the whites normally.

Because postural dialogs and spotting predators are key activities, horses have evolved an uncommonly large field of vision. With his head down in a grazing position, a horse can see about 350°, depending on the size and shape of the eye and jaw—everywhere but directly under his nose and behind his tail. A horse compensates for the blind spot directly behind him by having powerful hind legs and an instinctive tendency to kick at or run from whoever or whatever surprises him from the rear.

Each eye sees a different field of view, but horses do have 65–80° of binocular vision in the front. (Humans have about 130°, which is most of our visual field.) Horses have about the same depth perception as a cat or pigeon, and they can accurately judge distance and width using only one eye. The author once owned a mare that lost the sight of her right eye as a young filly; as an adult she had no trouble gauging the height or distance of jumps.

A horse can distinguish details at a distance about as well as a person with 20/33 vision. This is better than a dog (20/50) or cat (20/100). Kirkpatrick notes that the horse can recognize some objects at a great distance, noticing other horses as far as 2 mi/3.2 km away! A horse has excellent night vision with which to escape nocturnal predators and can navigate challenging terrain in what looks to a rider like total darkness. They cannot, however, see with great clarity in low light.

Horses can see color, but only about as much as a human being with red-green color blindness. A number of studies suggest that horses can readily distinguish orange, yellow, and blue from gray, but have trouble distinguishing red and green.

Horses communicate primarily with visual signals—body language and very small movements of the head, ears, and eyes—although they do use their voices as well. When horses meet, they exchange information that may be so subtle as to be inapparent to a human observer. These communications usually establish which horse is dominant. In general, the horse who wins the most conflicts is dominant and is entitled to more and better forage, first access to water, and more opportunities to reproduce.

Aggression usually begins as subtle nose-wrinkling and flattened ears. If these understated threats are ignored, the altercation escalates to head tossing, bared teeth, tail swishing, stamping a foreleg, charging, and biting. A horse on the defensive will use the same signals of nose-wrinkling and ear-flattening, along with tail-flattening and presenting the rump, backing toward the aggressor and swinging a hind hoof in a kick threat, or back-kicking with one or both hind hooves.

Submissive horses usually escape aggression by turning their heads away or by yielding space, withdrawing with ears half-flattened. If the threat comes from behind, the horse will tuck her tail and drop her croup as she retreats. Many horse trainers consider licking, chewing, and head-lowering submissive signals, but some scientists believe these behaviors are a displacement activity that occurs when horses experience conflicting impulses.

Yawning is also a displacement behavior, serving to release tension when the animal is conflicted. When humans approach too closely, barrier island horses often yawn, showing that they feel uncomfortable with the visitor, but not to the point of fight or flight. Keiper (1985) describes a mare yawning while standing over her dead foal, unsure whether she should stay with him.

Behavioral rules are somewhat lax for foals. Most of the time, elders patiently tolerate a youngster's inquisitive peskiness; but when tempers flare, an impatient kick can be lethal to a foal. To circumvent this risk, foals adopt a posture similar to an exaggerated nursing position—neck and muzzle extended, ears out to the sides, with the corners of the mouth drawn back and jaw clapping, as if trying to chew a thick chunk of bubble gum. Some interpret this snapping or champing as a ritualized version of the posture a horse takes in mutual grooming activity. This gesture was once thought to shut off aggressive tendencies in mature horses, translating as "Don't hurt me, I'm only a little baby!" Crowell-Davis found that snapping did not inhibit aggression and in some cases *caused* it (Crowell-Davis, Houpt, & Burnham, 1985). If champing is a submissive gesture, it is an inefficient one. It may be that champing is a displacement behavior derived from nursing that has a calming effect mainly on the horse doing the champing.

The set of the mouth communicates emotion. When a horse is tense, a deep triangle becomes visible above the mouth, the lips tighten, and the chin may dimple. Intense dislike or irritation is conveyed by wrinkling the mouth and nostrils. A relaxed horse may have droopy lips, ears, and eyelids. A contented horse may open its mouth slightly to expose the incisors and gums, with nostrils dilated, ears up

A horse's posture communicates volumes to the other horses in the herd. This Cumberland Island mare (center) moved the 2-year-old stallion (left) away from her foal by flattening her ears, raising and tossing her head, moving backwards, and shifting the weight off a hind leg. The juvenile stallion did not question her authority, but yielded ground by moving away until she dropped her threat, head low and tail clamped. If he had not moved fast or far enough, the mare would have followed with a series of forceful kicks or would have whirled to chase or bite the young stallion. Her foal presses close for her protection; his posture and the set of his ears indicate that he is curious and relaxed, but aware of the potential for danger. The foal to the right, who had been playing with the young stallion before the mare moved him away, watched attentively with concern but not fear. He was ready to move if the mare threatened him, but knew she was unlikely to unleash full violence on a young foal.

and forward, and a look of contentment in the eye. When scratching themselves on a branch or a stump, horses show pleasure by elongating the lips with half-closed eyes.

Keeping order on the move requires a great deal of communication. Horses communicate among themselves almost constantly, but the majority of their messages are silent, with occasional sounds that add emphasis or information. Most movies and television programs that feature horses dub inappropriate horse noises into the soundtrack, giving the impression that horses vocalize continually. Spending time with horses, one will quickly notice that they use their voices for only specific communications. Wild horses vocalize far less than domestic horses, particularly in herds where predators are a threat. Horses evolved on grasslands, and herd members usually remain in sight of one another at all times. The flattened ears and head toss of an irate mare is as effective as any vocalization and is less likely to draw the attention of predators.

The precise meaning of a vocalization is often related to context. The whinny is a loud call that carries over long distances. It can be used as a greeting, a call for a lost herd member, an invitation, or a plea for assistance. Stallions have a laugh-like, animated neigh when hopeful of romantic escapades and may trumpet, scream, or grunt when interacting with rival stallions.

The nicker is a low, soft sound that flutters through the nostrils, usually heard when a horse likes or wants something. Stallions and mares nicker in courtship. Mares nicker to foals. Domestic horses nicker when they hear grain rattle into a feed bucket.

A squeal expresses simultaneous fear and aggression. A mare will squeal when rejecting a stallion's advances or when protecting her foal. Horses meeting for the first time often sniff each other's breath intently, then squeal and strike out with a front hoof. Stallions sizing each other up have squealing contests. The longer, louder squeal usually belongs to the dominant animal.

Horses have an excellent sense of smell and frequently sniff objects or other horses. We do not know much about how they process this information. Two horses greeting each other will often softly blow into each other's nostrils. (Horses are unable to breathe through the mouth.) Stallions will greet other stallions and mares by sniffing at the flanks or elbow regions, then sniffing at the genitals—all areas rich with sweat glands and olfactory information, though what it means to the horse is anyone's guess.

Soon after birth, a foal will respond to a pungent aroma by curling back the upper lip in a flehmen posture, using another odor-sensing structure, the vomeronasal organ, deep within the nasal passages. Stallions use the flehmen posture to determine whether a mare is in heat, muzzle held high on an extended neck.

A horse compensates for the blind spot under his nose with incredibly sensitive lips and whiskers and an excellent sense of smell and taste. A domestic horse, given a mixture of pelleted dewormer and grain in which all particles are the same size, can eat just the grain, leaving the medicine behind. He can sort extraordinarily small things

Two horses in the Ocracoke Pony Pen communicate without making a sound. Lawton Howard, left, peers around the corner curiously before approaching to investigate a new visitor. Lindeza, right, is uncertain whether she should welcome the stranger. The set of her neck, head, and ears denotes uncertainty, and presenting her hind legs toward the photographer may denote insecurity.

with his lips. His olfactory acuity allows him to sniff a pile of manure and know immediately which horse deposited it or sniff a trail and determine which way his herdmates went.

Like people, horses are emotionally invested in knowing where they fit into a social hierarchy. After engaging in behaviors that establish dominance—flattened ears, biting, rearing, kicking, striking—the winning horse will often will often lay its head on the loser's rump, and by tolerating this gesture the loser accepts subordinate status. A stallion will also lay his head on a mare's rump before mounting, a final test of receptivity before moving into a more vulnerable position.

A frightened horse may sweat profusely, clamp his tail, raise his head, shift weight onto his hindquarters, and roll his eyes. Horses show annoyance or apprehension by twitching or wringing their tails or by stamping or pawing with their front feet. A horse may extend its upper lip in response to pleasurable sensations such as grooming or painful sensations like a bite on the hindquarters.

A horse's skin is very sensitive—he can respond to the sensation of a single fly walking on his neck or a rider's subtle shift of weight. Horses discourage biting flies by using the "fly-shaker" muscle, which rapidly twitches the skin surface and dislodges insects. When harassed by flies, they also stamp their front feet, shake their heads and necks to mobilize the mane, "cow-kick" at the belly with a hind hoof, or shake like a wet dog, legs apart and neck extended forward. A horse's tail is a supreme fly swatter, and it flicks constantly at the hindquarters and legs when insects are fierce. During fly season, horses often stand nose-to-tail with a friend, tails flicking over faces to keep biting insects at bay. Foals thrust their faces under their mothers' swishing tails for fly relief.

Rubenstein and Hohmann (1989) wrote that on Shackleford Banks, up to 200 flies can be found on a single horse. Flies bite adults in preference to juveniles, stallions in preference to mares, and dominant mares in preference to subordinates (probably because dominant mares stay closer to the stallions). Members of larger bands are bothered by fewer flies than horses in smaller groups, but flies are present in larger numbers on clusters of densely packed horses.

Horses dislodge insects and itchy, shedding hair by rubbing against branches and tree trunks, rubbing the face and eyes against the legs, or using the hind foot to scratch the head and ears. Foals self-groom much more often than mature horses, up to 12 times an hour between 5 and 8 weeks of age. A horse with pinworms (*Oxyuris equi*, different from human pinworms) may rub much of the hair off his tail head in response to anal itching.

Horses also roll on the ground to scratch itches, kill insects, and groom their coats. The horse begins by locating the perfect wallow of fine dirt, sand, or snow with few rocks or roots. He usually lowers his head, sniffs the ground, paws, and circles several times. Then he folds his front legs, followed by the hind legs, tips over onto his side, and rolls up toward his back. He rocks back and forth several times, and if he is fit and coordinated, he may flip himself over and attend to the opposite side. Some horses unable or unwilling to flip will stand, then lie down again on the opposite side to complete the process. When he is done, he will roll onto his chest, thrust his forelegs in front of him, and lurch upwards while getting his hind legs beneath him. Then he adopts a sawhorse posture, extends his nose and neck, and shakes off

Visitors can usually watch horses grazing and interacting in the front paddocks of the Ocracoke Pony Pen. Here, Little Doc, the 1986 son of Cubanito and Old Paint, crops the spring grass within his enclosure. He is a full brother to Lindeza.

the loose dirt. Most horses prefer to roll in sand or dry soil, but some prefer mud or even water.

Rolling is a contagious behavior, and other horses often follow suit, using the same wallow to scratch their own hides. The most dominant horse usually rolls last so its scent prevails. Other behaviors are socially contagious as well. Horses may defecate or urinate at the sight of a herdmate doing the same.

When one horse lies down to rest, others often do, too; but at least one horse usually remains standing on sentry duty. Most spend around 2 hours out of every 24 on their chests or flat on their sides for deeper sleep. Horses sleep efficiently standing up and doze this way for an hour or more at a time. Horse legs are constructed to lock into place for light sleep, so remaining upright requires minimal muscular effort.

Horses may vocalize or kick and make running movements during REM sleep. Stallions appear to have erotic dreams and may masturbate on waking (Houpt, 2005). Dreaming occurs only while the horse is recumbent because REM (rapid-eye-movement) sleep is accompanied by muscle relaxation so profound, that if he were standing he would fall over. Each dream cycle lasts only 3–10 minutes. Horses deprived of the opportunity to lie down for REM sleep by flooding, harassment by predators, or lack of companions to stand watch can suffer sleep deprivation, even to the point of narcoleptic collapse.

Physiologically, it is more stressful for a horse to sleep lying down because of increased pressure on internal organs, so horses are recumbent for only short intervals. Young foals spend almost half their time sleeping and do most of it on the ground. In the first two months of life, they spend 70–80% of their total resting time lying down. Foals spend half their time sleeping, usually sprawled flat on their sides. The average wild horse spends about 5 hr a day standing at rest, with one hind leg cocked, head down, in light sleep.

Although harem mares sleep 20–27% of the time, dominant stallions spend only 5–6% of their time asleep (Bennett & Hoffman, 1999). Horses sleep mostly at night and spend about 30–40% of the hours of darkness sleeping. Like new human mothers, mares with newborn foals get significantly less sleep.

A horse's daytime activities include grazing and grooming, seeking shade, and avoiding insects. During the summer, about 71% of daylight hours are spent grazing, which increases to 86% during the winter. Harem stallions become lean and mean during breeding season, spending 25–45% of their time in motion. Other herd members focus on resting or grazing and are active less than 10% of the time.

Keiper and Keenan (1980) observed that Assateague Ponies typically seek water just after sunset, then graze until about 10 p.m. During the evening they migrate from the marsh to preferred resting areas on hummocks supporting stands of pine and oak, on the dunes overlooking the ocean, or on the beach. Ponies are more likely to rest standing between 10 p.m. and midnight and from 3 a.m. to 4 a.m. Ponies are more likely to lie down to rest between midnight and 3 a.m., and about 4 a.m. embark on another round of grazing until after sunrise.

A horse typically produces manure every 75–90 min while feeding and every 3 hr when resting. Horses can defecate not only while walking, but also while trotting or even galloping. When one horse defecates, another often follows. Mares and prepubescent foals pass manure at random and urinate every 3–4 hr on average. Horses will often use a latrine area and avoid feeding on manured grass. Horses

An Assateague mare naps on the beach mid-day amid beach-goers. Barrier island horses often sleep on the beach during the summer to avoid biting flies, and to take advantage of the cooling sea breeze.

prefer to pass their water over an absorbent material such as grass or sand, because most dislike the splashing of urine on their legs.

For a stallion during the breeding season, urination and defecation are almost always socially significant. Whenever one of his mares urinates, the herd stallion sniffs it, lifts his lip in the flehmen posture to determine her estrus status, and then urinates over the spot. Marking is done more frequently if the mare is in heat—stallion urine contains pungent chemicals, including p-cresol, that disguise the scent of her receptivity from other stallions. Urine from mares in estrus evidently contains about half the p-cresol as that of stallions or non-receptive mares. When the stallion marks the urine of a mare in heat, the p-cresol in his urine appears to balance the shortage in hers, effectively disguising her status.

Horses have an amazingly acute sense of smell, and scent-marking is one of the few ways they can leave messages for other horses. If another stallion encounters this spot, he would inevitably sniff the mare's manure, and probably conclude "A mare was here, but she is claimed by this particular stallion."

The Ocracoke horses are now sheltered in a sturdy barn, but during the years when they ran wild, they had no protection from the elements. Horses in cool climates grow thick coats that provide insulation beginning in August or September and begin to shed their winter pelage when temperatures exceed 42°F/6°C. Loose hair begins to shed from the head and neck, then proceeds sequentially to the hindquarters, flank, back, front of the legs, and finally to the belly and insides of the legs. Within about 56 days, the horse has a slick, shiny summer coat. Yearlings can take up to 75 days to complete the process, presumably because nature better insulates babies against their first winter.

Coat density is individualized to an animal's needs: old, young, and very thin horses keep their winter coats longer because they have more difficulty staying warm. Foals born in late summer or fall have denser coats than those born in mid-spring.

The winter coat has a fine, springy undercoat to trap body heat and an outer layer of guard hairs that channels water off the horse. The mane, forelock, and long hairs under the jaw and down the legs also serve to channel water. When a horse is standing in the rain, his skin usually remains dry as the water runs off and the oily undercoat repels moisture.

Horses' winter coat is so heavy, coarse, and insulating, snow can remain on their backs without melting. Ice storms, however, can foil the animal's natural defenses and cause rapid heat loss. Ponies that have evolved in cold climates tend to have low-set tails, which allow snow to slide off the fan of hair at the top of the tail. During storms, horses turn their tails to the wind to conserve heat. Horses also conserve heat in cold weather by warming air through the large nasal sinuses before it enters the lungs, and they dissipate heat in hot weather by flaring their nostrils and breathing fast. Horses can generate heat by shivering.

The whiskers of the muzzle are easily mistaken for part of the hair coat, but in fact they are very responsive sense organs called vibrissae, with a rich nerve supply that may even detect sound. In mice, every whisker maps to its own region of sensory cortex in the brain, and it is quite possible the same is true of horses. If a portion of the brain is dedicated to processing information from each of these whiskers, the information they convey is probably more complex and valuable than we realize. At the very least, they communicate such information as the type of plants in front of the muzzle in the horse's blind spot and the distance of the muzzle from a surface. It has been

Horses graze the grasses that taste good nearly to the ground, nibble on other plants, and avoid eating bitter, toxic weeds such as buttercups. In a natural setting, horses graze for a short time, then move onto another section of their home range to allow the grass to grow back. In the pony pen, horses mow the greenery irregularly.

proposed that show horses are more likely to sustain facial trauma during trailer transport if they have had their whiskers removed for cosmetic purposes.

Equus has thrived for more than 4 million years mainly by virtue of adaptive behaviors that enhance the odds of staying alive long enough to reproduce. To a wild horse, anything unanticipated could threaten survival. Horses, wild and domestic, notice subtle changes in the environment and react to what they do not expect. Contrary to the opinion of many unseated riders, horses' skittishness does not denote stupidity. Horses do not always recognize danger immediately, so the equine strategy is to panic first, then sort out the details later. This could save his life.

Horses instinctively respond to movement. A noisy bird that launches suddenly from the trail ahead may panic a horse, which, for a moment, does not know that the sudden movement was not caused by a predator. Excitability to motion also means that if one horse bolts, the others in the vicinity bolt, too, or risk becoming a predator's next meal.

How does equine intellect compare to what humans call intelligence? Intelligence is hard to quantify or define in people and harder still to measure in other species. We tend to consider an animal intelligent if it behaves as we would in similar circumstances. Horses have evolved to survive in their ecological niche and would not have endured long if they were not well-suited to the task. To the non-horseman, however, equine quirks can seem erratic and irrational.

To survive in the wild, free-ranging horses must learn and remember their social, biological, and physical environments, including circumstances that change predictably at times and not at other times. For both wild and domestic horses, almost every activity of daily life involves cognition, learning, and memory. Horses with the greatest capacity to learn, understand, and solve problems are most likely to survive and reproduce.

Horses perform respectably, but not brilliantly, in studies involving mazes and do not rank high in reasoning or problem-solving ability. These skills are better developed in carnivores, which gained an evolutionary advantage by anticipating the movements of prey.

Horses are, however, extremely sharp when it comes to distinguishing differences, associating cues, and remembering associations. One study involving horses choosing symbols on LCD screens—large versus small, solid circle versus hollow, Snuffleupagus versus Cookie Monster—demonstrated that they could remember relatively complex problem-solving strategies for a minimum of 7–10 years and use these experiences to work out new challenges of a comparable nature.

Aside from the Shackleford and Corolla horses used to expand the gene pool of the herd, all the horses within Ocracoke's Pony Pen were born in captivity and raised on pasturage supplemented by hay and grain. Breedings are carefully planned to maximize the gene pool. Stallions are kept in separate paddocks, and males not chosen for breeding are gelded. The Park Service has protected Ocracoke from development and has preserved its natural beauty, but the island horses are no longer wild.

The advance of the modern world has pushed numerous strains of the wild Colonial Spanish Horse to the brink of extinction. The wild herds at Corolla and Shackleford and the captive herd at Ocracoke struggle to maintain genetically viable populations. Wild horses of old Spanish bloodlines once lived on islands all along the Southeastern

Lawton Howard, a friendly bay pinto gelding, comes to the fence to solicit attention from visitors. Lawton, a son of Santiago, is closely related to many of the horses in the herd and therefore was ineligible for the Park Service breeding program. He was gelded as a colt.

coast, from Florida to Virginia. Some breeds are no longer wild, but conservators have established breeding farms to preserve them.

The Cracker Horse of Florida and the Marsh Tacky of South Carolina and Georgia are breeds of old Spanish blood derived from wild horses that were re-domesticated. The Florida Cracker Horse (known variously as Seminole Pony, Prairie Pony, Florida Horse, Florida Cow Pony, and Grass Gut) was once abundant on the barrier islands of that state, but is no longer wild and is in danger of extinction. It appears that these horses derive not from the original Spanish expeditions, but from the Spanish settlements that came later. The Spanish brought the ancestors of Cracker Horses to Florida during the colonial period and put them to use working cattle on their ranches. The name of the breed is said to derive from the cracking of the cowboys' bullwhips. When the Dust Bowl desiccated the Western rangelands, stockmen drove their cattle to the lush pastures of Florida, thus introducing more Western horses. The task of roping and holding cattle required a larger, stronger horse, and the Spanish Cracker was replaced by the Quarter Horse, which by this time was a taller and heavier breed.

The Marsh Tacky of South Carolina and Georgia was once the most abundant horse in the Low Country. Today the American Livestock Breeds Conservancy believes that there are fewer than 150 pure Marsh Tackies left. Breeders carefully plan matings to preserve the integrity of the breed—some bloodlines have remained pure since the Civil War era. Like the closely related Banker Pony, the Marsh Tacky has been protected from dilution by geographic isolation, so it has retained many strong Spanish characteristics. Tackies are renowned for their intelligence, ruggedness, and kind dispositions.

Wild-horse rehabilitator Steve Edwards (2011) admires the tough little horses:

> I love Marsh Tackies. They are now the state horse of South Carolina, as they should be. Their history is intricately bound with the history of working people from the Low Country to the Mountains. Small, gaited, remarkably calm, trainable and tough—endless endurance. . . .
>
> Like the Bankers, they were the horses of poor, hardworking folks. Indeed, the breed name "Tacky" is rooted in its Colonial meaning, not as being of poor quality but of being common and widespread. Today they are neither common nor widespread. Like the Corollas, their future is very tenuous.

The Florida Cracker, the Marsh Tacky, and the horses of the Outer Banks are considered Colonial Spanish Horses based on conformation and genetic makeup and are worthy of preservation as unique herds with genetic, historic, and cultural value. They are recognized as among the few remaining vestiges of the ancient Spanish Jennet.

Numerous strains of Colonial Spanish Horses have died out over the years, their genes lost forever. The Ocracoke Ponies were headed down a similar path until people stepped in to save them from extinction. Despite their low numbers, Ocracoke horses show no signs of inbreeding depression, due to introductions from outside horses.

Recently, the Park Service has brought in horses from Shackleford Banks and Corolla to benefit the genetic health of the herd and to breed the Ocracoke horses back toward their historic bloodlines. Cothran (personal communication, April 20, 2011) said,

They are reasonably good sources of additional variability. Possibly all of the horses on the Outer Banks share some ancestry, [from] the Shackleford Banks and Carrot Island up to a little population in Virginia at Back Bay. You can maintain variability at a much higher level with as little as one effective migrant per generation. It doesn't take much crossing to restore the variability.

Historically, people have "improved" feral herds by introducing outside stallions, reasoning that one male horse can sire many offspring with many mares throughout his lifetime. Unfortunately, his fecundity can hijack the gene pool and eliminate the characteristics of the original herd. Cothran cautions,

> I usually recommend that you use mares if you are going to make exchanges, if you're trying to preserve the particular characteristics of a population. The reason is that they will have less impact on the population, yet they will, over time, help the variability to recover. Within a feral population in the Theodore Roosevelt National Park [North Dakota], fully 15% of that gene pool was from one introduced stallion, and that percentage is probably going to increase over time. He was a very dominant type of stallion. The local people had introduced big horses in there to create bucking stock for rodeos. This was a big horse—and he was very effective. (Personal communication, April 20, 2011)

In December 2009, Cape Hatteras NS adopted Sacajawea and Jitterbug, young Shackleford mares who will contribute their genes to the Ocracoke herd. Two privately owned Shackleford stallions, Wenzel and Doran, are on loan.

In 2010, Wenzel, the size of a Welsh pony, was cohabiting with Maya, at 15.2 hands (62 in./1.57 m) the tallest horse in the herd. Wenzel had to climb onto a manger to consummate the union. There was a similar height disparity between Doran and his mate Luna. Soon after his arrival on Ocracoke, Wenzel impregnated Spirit, one of the younger mares in the herd. In March 2010 she delivered Paloma. Alonzo, a 3-year-old sorrel Corolla stallion, joined the herd in 2012.

Santiago is an 18-year-old pinto stallion with contrasting irregular markings, long flowing mane and tail, and strikingly Spanish conformation. He is the sire of four mares and one gelding within the herd.

Tall ladies are not a problem! Luna, a gray mare who was born a pinto, shares a nuzzle with her diminutive stallion Doran over the manger. Luna is uncommonly tall for a Banker horse, standing 15 hands (60 in./1.52 m). Her height and gray coloring apparently trace to Cubanito, an Andalusian stallion introduced into the Ocracoke herd in the 1970s. At 12.2 hands, Doran is about typical in size for a Shackleford.

Breedings are carefully planned to increase genetic diversity, but sometimes animal instinct trumps science. Some years ago, Jim, a 25-year-old Banker stallion of the original bloodlines, was diagnosed with cancer. The rangers attempted to breed him with Nevada and Lindessa, but after consorting with him for months, their pregnancy tests came back negative. One day that spring, Ranger Bill Caswell went to the pony pen and saw something small and brown in the pasture. Nevada had delivered a foal unexpectedly during the night. The ponies are largely named by local school children. For this filly, they selected *Bonita Sopresa*, Spanish for "Beautiful Surprise."

One mare, chestnut with a white snip, was conceived after her sire escaped from his corral and had a romantic interlude with her dam. The mare's name? Oops. As a mature mare, Oops went on to cohabit with Santiago for two years, but the rangers never saw them mate.

One morning Park Service volunteer Kimberly Emery arrived to feed the horses and found that Oops had unexpectedly delivered a handsome pinto colt. He was named Lawton Howard in honor of a beloved island native who had died in 2002. Lawton is a healthy,

Sacajawea, a young Shackleford mare, joined the Ocracoke herd in December 2009. The Park Service hopes that her offspring will breathe new life into the Ocracoke herd.

sociable gelding who loves to be the center of attention, persistently soliciting scratching, stroking, and praise from Ranger Laura Michaels, their handler. Michaels, who vacationed on Ocracoke as a child, took a job with the Park Service as a seasonal maintenance worker in 2001. She tended the ponies three times weekly as a volunteer. Seven years later, she was awarded a permanent position as the official Ocracoke wrangler.

Ocracoke's Banker ponies remain on site as memento of what was. Though no longer free to run the beaches in great numbers as their ancestors did for centuries, their confinement does not diminish their importance. Some, however, feel that their importance should diminish their confinement. Restricted to less than 4% of Ocracoke's federal land, this herd is too small to survive without infusions of outside blood. To become self-sustaining, the horses would require greater access to their historic range.

The Banker ponies of Ocracoke represent a rare strain of a rare breed that nearly vanished, and one of the last vestiges of an important aspect of Outer Banks history. Their future remains uncertain. In 2010, there were 21 horses in the Ocracoke herd, and only five mares of breeding age. Most of the reproductively eligible females seem to have fertility issues and remain barren despite access to stallions. When the author visited the herd in 2009, there was a large contingent of elderly horses: Mr. Bob (33) Okies Rainbow (31), Nevada (28) and South Wind (28).

In 2014, the census was 18, and the herd was becoming more genetically diverse, yet truer to its historic lineage. Paloma was foaled in 2010, and two two years later her full sibling was born—a seal brown pinto colt named Rayo, or 'thunderbolt.' In May, 2013, Jitterbug, born on Shackleford Banks, and Alonzo, born on Currituck Banks, became parents to a chestnut colt named Captain Marvin Howard by local school children. This new generation lifts the hearts of countless devotees who fervently hope that this rare breed will survive the challenges ahead.

Hoofprints Guide

References

An Act To Provide for the Removal of Cattle Remaining on Core Banks in Carteret County. (1959). NC Sess L 1959 ch 782.

Almendrala, A. (2012, May 16.) Horse named 'Air of Temptation' runs into sea, is rescued a mile from shore. *The Huffington Post*. Retrieved from http://www.huffingtonpost.com/2012/05/16/horse-runs-into-sea-rescu_n_1521798.html

American Livestock Breeds Conservancy. (2009). *Conservation priority equine breeds 2009*. Retrieved from http://www.albc-usa.org/documents/ALBCEquineCPL.pdf

Avitable, J. (2009). *The Atlantic world economy and colonial Connecticut* (Unpublished doctoral dissertation). University of Rochester, NY.

Bank of England. (n.d.). *Inflation calculator*. Retrieved from http://www.bankofengland.co.uk/education/Pages/inflation/calculator/flash/default.aspx

Barnes, J. (2007, November-December). Scattered by the wind: The lost settlement of Diamond City. *Weatherwise, 60*(6), 36–41. doi: 10.3200/WEWI.60.6.36-41

Battling stallions run Banker ponies off Ocracoke Isle. (1951, June 5). *Evening Telegram* (Rocky Mount, NC), p. 3B.

Bennett, D., & Hoffman, R.S. (1999, December). *Equus caballus. Mammalian Species, 628*, 1–14.

Beranger, J. (2009). *The Marsh Tacky Horse—Yesterday and today*. Retrieved from http://blackberryridgehorsefarm.com/history_of_the_marsh_tacky_horse.html

Berenger, R. (1771). *The history and art of horsemanship*. London, United Kingdom: For T. Davies and T. Cadell.

Brooks, B. (1956, March). Riders of the beach. *Boy's Life, 46*(3), 25–26, 69.

Browne, D.J. (1854). Domestic animals. In C. Mason, *Report of the Commissioner of Patents for the year 1853: Agriculture* (S. Ex. Doc. 27, 33rd Congress, 1st Session) (pp. 1–4). Washington, DC: Beverley Tucker.

Cameron, E.Z., Setsaas, T.H., & Linklater, W.L. (2009). Social bonds between unrelated females increase reproductive success in feral horses. *Proceedings of the National Academy of Sciences of the United States of America, 106*(33), 13850–13853. doi: 10.1073/pnas.0900639106

Sam Jones, Ocracoke, 1956. Photograph from the Aycock Brown Collection, Outer Banks History Center.

Chadwick v. Salter, 254 N.C. 389, 119 S.E.2d 158 (1961).

Chard, T. (1940). Did the first Spanish horses landed in Florida and Carolina leave progeny? *American Anthropologist, 42*(1), 90–106. doi: 10.1525/aa.1940.42.1.02a00060

Chater, M. (1926). Motor-coaching through North Carolina. *National Geographic, 49* (5), 475–523.

Conant, E.K., Juras, R., & Cothran, E.G. (2012). A microsatellite analysis of five colonial Spanish horse populations of the southeastern United States. *Animal Genetics, 43*(1), 53–62. doi: 10.1111/j.1365-2052.2011.02210.x

Cooper J.F. (1831). *The last of the Mohicans; A narrative of 1757.* London, United Kingdom: Henry Colburn & Richard Bentley.

Cothran, E.G. (2011, April 20). Personal communication

Crowell-Davis, S.L., & Weeks, J.W. (2005). Maternal behavior and mare-foal interaction. In D.S. Mills & S.M. McDonnell, *The domestic horse: The evolution, development, and management of its behavior* (pp. 126–138). Cambridge, United Kingdom: Cambridge University Press.

Crowell-Davis, S.L., Houpt, K.A., & Burnham, J.S. (1985). Snapping by foals of *Equus caballus. Zeitschrift für Tierpsychologie, 69*(1), 42–54. doi: 10.1111/j.1439-0310.1985.tb00755.x

Culver, F.B. (1922). *Blooded horses of colonial days: Classic horse matches in America before the Revolution.* Baltimore, MD: Author.

"D." (1832). A list of all the stallions that have stood along the Roanoke, in the state of North Carolina, from the Revolution to the present time. *American Turf Register and Sporting Magazine, 3*(6), 272–277.

Dallaire, A., & Ruckebusch, Y. (1974, January). Sleep and wakefulness in the housed pony under different dietary conditions. *Canadian Journal of Comparative Medicine, 38*(1), 65–71. Retrieved from http://www.ncbi.nlm.nih.gov/pmc/articles/PMC1319968/pdf/compmed00045-0071.pdf

Federation of Animal Science Societies. (2010, January). *Guide for the care and use of agricultural animals in research and teaching* (3rd ed.). Champaign, IL: Author. Retrieved from http://www.fass.org/docs/agguide3rd/Chapter08.pdf

Dodge, T. A. (1892). The horse in America. *North American Review, 155*(433), 667–683.

Du Bois, W.E.B. (1896). *The suppression of the African slave trade to the United States of America, 1638–1870.* Harvard Historical Studies. New York, NY: Longmans, Green, and Co.

Dunbar, G.S. (1958). *Historical geography of the North Carolina Outer Banks.* Louisiana State University Studies, Coastal Studies Series 3. Baton Rouge: Louisiana State University Press.

Dunbar, G.S. (1961). Colonial Carolina cowpens. *Agricultural History, 35*(3), 125–131.

Eaton, L. (1989). The last of the Currituck Beach cowboys. *Outer Banks Magazine,* 1989–1990 annual, 22–27, 83–84.

Edwards, S. (2010, March 10). They look smaller up close. *Mill Swamp Indian Horse Views.* Retrieved from http://msindianhorses.blogspot.com/2010/03/they-look-smaller-up-close.html

Edwards, S. (2011, December 16). High on the hog—putting 'Cuz to work. *Mill Swamp Indian Horse Views.* Retrieved from http://msindianhorses.blogspot.com/2011/12/high-on-hog-putting-cuz-to-work.html

Ellenberger, W.P., & Chapin, R.M. (1919). *Cattle-fever ticks and methods of eradication* (Farmers' Bulletin 1057). Washington, DC: U. S. Department of Agriculture. Retrieved from http://books.google. com/books/download/Cattle_fever_ticks_and_methods_of_ eradic.pdf?id=JCkbAAAAYAAJ&output=pdf&sig=ACfU3U270H G8hGj4IKNtsQa6ESByhTJt2Q

Engels, W.L. (1942). Vertebrate fauna of North Carolina coastal islands: A study in the dynamics of animal distribution I. Ocracoke Island. *American Midland Naturalist, 28*(2), 273–304.

Feh, C. (2005). Relationships and communication in socially natural horse herds. In D.S. Mills & S.M. McDonnell (Eds.), *The domestic horse: The origins, development and management of its behaviour* (pp. 83–109). Cambridge, United Kingdom: Cambridge University Press.

Gill, E. (1994). *Ponies in the wild.* London, United Kingdom: Whittet Books.

Goerch, C. (1995). *Ocracoke.* Winston-Salem, NC: John F. Blair (Original work published 1956 and revised in later printings).

[Goldsmith, O.] (1768). *The present state of the British Empire in Europe, America, Africa and Asia. . . .* London, United Kingdom: For W. Griffin, J. Johnson, W. Nicoll, and Richardson and Urquhart.

Goodwin, D. (2002). Horse behaviour: Evolution, domestication and feralisation. In N. Waran (Ed.), *The Welfare of Horses* (pp. 1–18). Dordrecht, Netherlands: Kluwer Academic Publishers.

Gregg, A. (1867). *History of the Old Cheraws: Containing an account of the aborigines of the Pedee, the first white settlements . . . extending from about A.D. 1730 to 1810. . . .* New York, NY: Richardson and Company.

Hall, S.J.G. (2005). The horse in human society. In D.S. Mills & S.M. McDonnell (Eds.), *The domestic horse: The origins, development and management of its behaviour* (pp. 23–32). Cambridge, United Kingdom: Cambridge University Press.

Hanggi, E., & Ingersoll, J. (2009). Long-term memory for categories and concepts in horses (*Equus caballus*). *Animal Cognition, 12*(3), 451–462. doi: 10.1007/s10071-008-0205-9

Harriot, T. (1590). *A briefe and true report of the new found land of Virginia.* Frankfurt-am-Main, Germany: Johann Wechel.

Harrison, F. (1929). *The Belair Stud, 1747–1761*. Richmond, VA: Old Dominion Press.

Harrison, F. (1931). *The John's Island Stud (South Carolina) 1750–1788*. Richmond, VA: Old Dominion Press.

Harrison, F. (1934). *Early American turf stock, 1730–1830* (Vol. 1). Richmond, VA: Old Dominion Press.

Henning, J. (1985). *Conquistadores' legacy: The horses of Ocracoke*. Ocracoke, NC: Author.

Herbert. H.W. (1857). *Horse and horsemanship and the United States and British provinces of North America* (Vol. 1). New York, NY: Stringer & Townsend.

Heyward, D., & Allen, H. (1922). *Carolina chansons: Legends of the Low Country*. New York, NY: MacMillan.

Houpt, K. (2005). Maintenance behaviours. In D.S. Mills & S.M. McDonnell (Eds.), *The domestic horse: The origins, development and management of its behaviour* (pp. 94–109). Cambridge, United Kingdom: Cambridge University Press.

Howard, M. (1976). Ocracoke horsemen. In C. O'Neal, A. Rondthaler, & A. Fletcher (Eds.), *The story of Ocracoke Island: A Hyde County bicentennial project* (pp. 25–27). Charlotte, NC: Herb Eaton.

Howard, P. (2002, May 1). *Ocracoke Newsletter*. Retrieved from http://www.village craftsmen.com/news050102.htm#top

Howren, R. (1962). The speech of Ocracoke, North Carolina. *American Speech, 37*(3), 163–175.

Impact Assessment, Inc. (2005). *Ethnohistorical description of the eight villages adjoining Cape Hatteras National Seashore and interpretive themes of history and heritage: Final technical report*. Manteo, NC: Cape Hatteras National Seashore.

Ives, V. (2007). *Corolla and Shackleford Horse of the Americas inspections—February 23–25, 2007*. Retrieved from http://www.corollawildhorses.com/Images/HOA Report/hoa-report.pdf

Keiper, R. (1985). *The Assateague ponies*. Atglen, PA: Schiffer Publishing.

Keiper, R.R., & Keenan, M.A. (1980). Nocturnal activity patterns of feral ponies. *Journal of Mammalogy, 61*(1), 116–118.

Kimura, R. (2001). Volatile substances in feces, urine and urine-marked feces of feral horses. *Canadian Journal of Animal Science, 81*(3), 411–420. doi: 10.4141/A00-068

Lee, F.G. (2008). *Constructing the Outer Banks: Land use, management, and meaning in the creation of an American place* (Unpublished master's thesis). North Carolina State University, Raleigh.

Little, M.R. (2012, April 24). *A comprehensive architectural survey of Carteret County, North Carolina's archipelago: Final report.* Raleigh, NC: Author.

Mallinson, D.J., Culver, S.J., Riggs, S.R., Walsh, J.P., Ames, D., & Smith, C.W. (2008). *Past, present and future inlets of the Outer Banks barrier islands, North Carolina.* Greenville, NC: East Carolina University.

Mallinson, D.J., Riggs, S.R., Culver, S.J., Ames, D., Horton, B.P., & Kemp, A.C. (2009). *The North Carolina Outer Banks barrier islands: A field trip guide to the geology, geomorphology, and processes.* Retrieved from http://core.ecu.edu/geology/mallinsond/ IGCP_NC_Field_Trip_Guide_rev1.pdf

McGreevy, P. (2004). *Equine behavior: A guide for veterinarians and equine scientists.* London, United Kingdom: W.B. Saunders.

Meader, S.W. (1959). *Wild pony island.* New York, NY: Harcourt, Brace.

Muhonen, S., & Lönn, M. (2003). *The behaviour of foals before and after weaning in group* (Examensarbete 190). Uppsala: Swedish University of Agricultural Sciences, Department of Animal Nutrition and Management.

Munsell, J.W. (1946, August 22). Hunting and fishing. *Newark Advocate* (Newark, NJ), p. 11.

Murphy, J., Hall, C., & Arkins, S. (2009). What horses and humans see: A comparative review. *International Journal of Zoology, 2009,* Article ID 721798. doi: 10.1155/ 2009/721798

Newsome, A.R. (1929, October). A miscellany from the Thomas Henderson letter book, 1810–1811. *North Carolina Historical Review,* 6, 398–410.

Nicholls, J. (Artist). (1736). Edward Teach commonly call'd Black Beard. In C. Johnson [Daniel Defoe], *A general history of the lives and adventures of the most famous highwaymen . . . to which is added, a genuine account of the voyages and plunders of the most notorious pyrates . . .* (plate facing p. 86). London, United Kingdom: Oliver Payne.

Nicol, C.J. (2005). Learning abilities in the horse. In D.S. Mills & S.M. McDonnell (Eds.), *The domestic horse: The origins, development and management of its behaviour* (pp. 169–183). Cambridge, United Kingdom: Cambridge University Press.

Norris, D.A. (2006). Shell Castle. *NCpedia*. Retrieved from http://ncpedia.org/shell-castle

Olszewski, G. (1970, September). *Historic resource study for history of Portsmouth Village, Cape Lookout National Seashore, North Carolina.* Retrieved from http://www.nps.gov/history/history/online_books/calo/portsmouth_village.pdf

O'Neal, C., Rondthaler, A., & Fletcher, A. (Eds.). (1976). *The story of Ocracoke Island: A Hyde County bicentennial project.* Charlotte, NC: Herb Eaton.

O'Neal, Jr., E.W. (2008). *Wild Ponies of Ocracoke Island, North Carolina.* Privately published.

Peck, K.J. (2008). *Horse husbandry in colonial Virginia: An analysis of probate inventories in relation to environmental and social changes* (Unpublished honors thesis). College of William and Mary, Williamsburg, VA.

Phillips, D. (1922, May). *Horse raising in colonial New England* (Cornell University Agricultural Experiment Station Memoir 54). Ithaca, NY: Cornell University.

Proops, L., & McComb, K. (2010). Attributing attention: The use of human-given cues by domestic horses (*Equus caballus*). *Animal Cognition, 13*(2), 197–205. doi: 10.1007/s10071-009-0257-5

Purchasing power of British pounds from 1245 to present. (2013). Retrieved from http://www.measuringworth.com/calculators/ppoweruk

Quinn, D.B. (Ed.) (1955). *The Roanoke voyages, 1584–1590: Documents to illustrate the English voyages to North America under the patent granted to Walter Raleigh in 1584.* London, United Kingdom: For the Hakluyt Society.

Ramsay, D. (1809). *The history of South-Carolina, from its first settlement in 1670 to the year 1808* (Vol. 2). Charleston, SC: David Longworth.

Remington, F. (1895, August). [Cracker Cowboys on horseback]. In Remington, F., Cracker Cowboys of Florida. *Harper's New Monthly Magazine, 91*(543), 339.

Rubenstein, D.I., & Hohmann, M.E. (1989). Parasites and social behavior of island feral horses. *Oikos, 55*(3), 312–320.

Ruffin, E. (1861). *Agricultural, geological, and descriptive sketches of lower North Carolina, and the similar adjacent lands.* Raleigh, NC: Institution for the Deaf & Dumb & the Blind.

Ryden, H. (2005). *America's last wild horses* (Revised ed.). New York, NY: Lyons Press.

Smith, J. (1624). *The generall historie of Virginia, New-England, and the Summer Isles.* London, England: Michael Sparkes.

Smyth, J.F.D. (1784). *A tour in the United States of America . . .* (Vol. 1). London, United Kingdom: For G. Robinson, J. Robson, & J. Sewell.

Sponenberg, D.P. (1992). The colonial Spanish horse in the USA: History and current status. *Archivos de Zootecnia, 41*(154/extra), 335–348. Retrieved from http://dialnet.unirioja.es/servlet/articulo?codigo=278710&orden=0& info=link

Sponenberg, D.P. (2011). *North American Colonial Spanish Horse update, July 2011.* Retrieved from http://www.centerforamericas-firsthorse.org/north-american-colonial-spanish-horse.html

Sponenberg, D.P. (2012, December 4). Personal communication.

Sponenberg, D.P., & Reed, C. (2009). Colonial Spanish type matrix. In U.S. Bureau of Land Management, Billings Field Office, *Pryor Mountain wild horse range herd management area plan and environmental assessment* (EA #MT-010-08-24) (pp. 140–143). Billings, MT: Bureau of Land Management, Billings Field Office.

Stevens, E.F. (1990). Instability of harems of feral horses in relation to season and presence of subordinate stallions. *Behaviour, 112*(3-4), 149–161. doi: 10.1163/156853990X00167

Stick, D. (1952). *Graveyard of the Atlantic: Shipwrecks of the North Carolina Coast.* Chapel Hill: University of North Carolina Press.

Stick, D. (1958). *The Outer Banks of North Carolina, 1584–1958.* Chapel Hill: University of North Carolina Press.

Thomas, J.E., Rhue, R.D., & Hornsby, A.G. (2009). *Arsenic contamination from cattle-dipping vats* (Publication SL 152). Gainesville: University of Florida Institute of Food and Agricultural Sciences. Retrieved from http://edis.ifas.ufl.edu/ss205

Turner, F. (n.d.). *Money and exchange rates in 1632.* Retrieved from http://www.google.com/search?q=pound+peso+exchange+rate+16th+century&rls=com.microsoft:en-us:IE-Address&ie=UTF-8&oe=UTF-8&sourceid=ie7&rlz=1I7ACEW_enUS482

U.S. Bureau of Labor Statistics. (n.d.). *CPI inflation calculator.* Retrieved from http://www.bls.gov/data/inflation_calculator.htm

Vegetation scarcity blamed on N.C. oceanside ponies. (1940, March 12). *Portsmouth Herald* (Portsmouth, VA), p. 10.

Wallace, J.H. (1897). *The horse of America in his derivation, history, and development.* New York, NY: Author.

Westvang, D. (2008). *Finding the foundation.* Retrieved from http://www.foxtrotterfoundation.com/FINDINGTHEFOUNDATION.doc

Welch, W. L. (1885). *An account of the cutting through of Hatteras Inlet, North Carolina, September 7, 1846. Also through which inlet did the English adventurers of 1584, enter the sounds of North Carolina and Some changes in the coast line since their time.* Salem, MA: Salem Press.

Winsor, J. (1886). *Narrative and critical history of North America* (Vol. 2, Spanish explorations and settlements in America from the fifteenth to the seventeenth century). Boston, MA: Houghton, Mifflin.

Wiss, Janney, Elstner Associates & John Milner Associates. (2007). *Portsmouth Village cultural landscape report*. Atlanta, GA: U.S. National Park Service, Southeast Regional Office. Retrieved from http://www.nps.gov/calo/parkmgmt/upload/CALO Portsmouth Village CLR_Site History.pdf

Acknowledgments

About 20 years ago, I began to research my first book, *Hoofprints in the Sand: Wild Horses of the Atlantic Coast*. The experience enriched my life in many ways. I learned a tremendous amount about how the natural behavior of these horses differs from that of their domestic counterparts. Following herds through marsh and dune, I gained a greater appreciation of the complexity of their apparently simple lives in the wild. Similarly, with the writing of *Wild Horse Dilemma*, many helpful and extraordinary people have earned my gratitude, and many have become friends.

Dr. Jay F. Kirkpatrick, senior scientist at the Science and Conservation Center at ZooMontana in Billings and author of *Into the Wind: Wild Horses of North America*, has devoted much of his career to preserving the health, rights, and dignity of wild horses. He developed and implemented the immunocontraceptive program in use with many species of wildlife, including horses. He answered my questions, forwarded useful documents, crafted an insightful preface, and generously reviewed the manuscript before publication.

Don Höglund, DVM, is an internationally esteemed leader in horse training and management and the author of *Nobody's Horses*, a riveting book about the rescue of wild horses from the White Sands Missile Range. He has implemented numerous large-scale equine programs, including the Department of the Interior's Wild Horse Prison Inmate Training Program, which teaches prisoners to gentle horses while providing training for adoptable mustangs. His love and admiration for horses is evident in all that he does. When I approached him with a few questions, he responded enthusiastically and sent me a number of articles that shaped the backbone of my manuscript. I am grateful for his support and encouragement along the way and fortunate that he agreed to review the manuscript.

Dr. E. Gus Cothran, Texas A&M University's renowned expert on the genetics of wild and domestic horses, helped me to understand the significance of the Q-ac variant in certain wild horse herds and the concept of minimum viable population. He also found time in his busy schedule to review the manuscript. His research is the cornerstone of wild horse management, and I have cited it extensively.

Dr. Sue Stuska, the wildlife biologist at Cape Lookout National Seashore who oversees the Shackleford Banks herd, has corresponded regularly about the status of the horses. When I visited, she taught me how to identify individuals, and showed me her dynamic census chart that tracks the members of each band and where they were last sighted. She explained how the current management plan makes optimal use of the existing gene pool by monitoring family lineage and contracepting certain mares. Sue also gave of her valuable time to review my manuscript for accuracy.

Doug Hoffman, wildlife biologist at Cumberland Island National Seashore, helped me to understand the Park Service perspective on the horses living there and corrected my assumptions and misinformation. He generously drove me to key parts of the island that I could not otherwise reach, and my time with him was the highlight of the trip.

Karen McCalpin, director of the nonprofit Corolla Wild Horse Fund, Inc., found time in her impossibly busy schedule to meet me and discuss the genetic crisis facing the herd. She also reviewed the manuscript. Karen and the other members of the organization—mostly volunteers—have upended their lives to secure protection for these horses. Karen produced a beautifully written blog highlighting the triumphs and tragedies of the herd. It can be accessed at www.corollawildhorses.com

Dr. Ronald Keiper, Distinguished Professor of Biology (emeritus) at Penn State University, was one of the first scientists to study the behavior of horses in the wild, answered my questions about the foaling rate of lactating mares and shared his groundbreaking research detailing the behavior of the Assateague horses.

Wesley Stallings, former manager of the Corolla herd, took me in his truck several times as he patrolled the Outer Banks north of Corolla, following the movements of wild bands and logging herd data in his notebook. Sometimes we climbed on the roof of the truck to scout for horses. Sometimes Wes climbed a tree for a better view. At one point we encountered a flooded hollow and were forced to don hip boots and slog through surging currents occupied by cottonmouth snakes

Pinto horses with unique markings cover a page in an informal scrapbook kept by the National Park Service. Many of the horses depicted lived and died decades ago.

to evaluate the health of a newborn colt. I am grateful he allowed me to participate in his daily adventures.

Steve Edwards, by day an attorney for Isle of Wight County, Virginia, works magic in rehabilitating injured Corolla and Shackleford horses. At his farm, Mill Swamp Indian Horses in Smithfield, Va., he teaches children how to train wild horses with natural horsemanship techniques. He also established an off-site breeding program to preserve the herd's rare genes in case of disaster in the wild. Steve has been extremely supportive and helpful throughout the writing of this book, and has brought his expertise to the task of reviewing this book for accuracy before publication.

In 2012, I visited Mill Swamp and was captivated by the sight of children working in the round pen with young horses, many of them recently brought in from the wild. To this point, I had great esteem for the wild horses living on North Carolina's Outer Banks, but had never ridden one. I found these Colonial Spanish Horses astonishingly surefooted, brave, rugged, and smooth-gaited. The climax of my visit was a ride through the inky forest astride Manteo, a wild-born black stallion. He never missed a step despite exposed roots, steep embankments, deep pools, and deer crashing gracelessly through the underbrush. For the better part of an hour, we trotted and cantered through darkness so complete, I could not see my hand in front of my face. I had recently been injured in a riding accident, and I was working through many horse-related fears. It was a profound and humbling experience to trust a once-wild stallion to find his way through darkness that left me blind.

D. Phillip Sponenberg, DVM, PhD, helped me to understand the genetic underpinnings of coat color and its implications for the free-roaming Banker horses. In his review of the manuscript, he offered great insights on Spanish horse origins and genetics, and his comprehensive articles on that topic were a valuable resource.

Carolyn Mason, president of the Foundation for Shackleford Horses, Inc., accompanied me to Shackleford Banks and generously shared her wealth of knowledge about the horses. She introduced me to the Banker Horses grazing in her yard, gentled animals awaiting adoption. My heart melted when a young gelding named Adagio followed me like a puppy and courted hugs and scratching.

Woody and Nena Hancock loaded me and my cameras into their boat and searched island and marsh for members of the Cedar Island herd. They introduced me to Bucky, the most genetically valuable horse on Cedar Island, and her 2-week-old look-alike filly, Gay; a mare who prefers the company of three burly wild bulls; and Shack, the robust sorrel patriarch whose photograph graces the front cover of this book. It was a profound, almost holy experience to stand calf-deep in warm estuarine waters under a moody sky, surrounded by peaceful wild horses, splashing pelicans, and wind-licked marsh grass.

Laura Michaels, the Park Service ranger in charge of pony care, took me behind the scenes to meet the Ocracoke horses. I also met Wenzel, Doran, Sacajawea, and Jitterbug, the Shackleford horses who will revitalize the Ocracoke herd. I even scratched the neck of the lovely black-and-white mare Easter Lady after admiring her from afar for years.

Roe Terry, former public relations specialist of the Chincoteague Volunteer Fire Company, invited me to the workshop where he carves graceful wooden waterfowl and discussed the challenges faced by the hardworking firefighters. Besides managing the herd of free-roaming ponies, these dedicated people donate their time to provide tax-free fire suppression, search and rescue, and emergency medical services in a town of 4,400 permanent residents that receives roughly 1.5 million visitors a year. He also granted me access to the optimal vantage point for the world-famous Chincoteague Pony Swim: whereas most onlookers stood in a field behind an orange fence, out of harm's way, I was able to stand directly on the grassy landing where the horses regained solid ground after swimming the channel from Chincoteague National Wildlife Refuge. Ponies rose out of the water like mythical creatures of the sea, dripping wet and looking very pleased with themselves. My feet were in their hoofprints, and occasionally I dove for cover as a stallion thundered by in pursuit of a rival. It was a magical experience.

Denise Bowden, his successor at the fire company, cheerfully supplied me with useful information. Her passion for the horses and the refuge are evident, and her enthusiasm enhances the overall festivity of Pony Penning week.

Lou Hinds, former manager of the Chincoteague NWR, took me around the refuge to show me unequivocal signs of dramatic environmental change, such as tree trunks, light poles, and chunks of peat that had once been on the bay side of Assateague until island migration situated them squarely on the beach. Studying the dynamic nature of barrier islands is one thing; seeing the evidence of their migration is another thing entirely.

Pam Emge, co-author of *Chincoteague Ponies: Untold Tails*, can identify all of the Chincoteague wild ponies and knows the intimate details of their relationships and lineages. She reviewed part of the manuscript, corrected errors, and filled in details.

Anthropologist Karen Dalke of the University of Wisconsin-Green Bay shared her doctoral dissertation and other writings, which provide unique perspective on what we feel about wild horses and how we define them. She also reviewed the manuscript prior to publication.

Paula Gillikin, manager of the Rachel Carson North Carolina National Estuarine Research Reserve, assisted me in researching the horses of Carrot Island and vicinity.

Philip Howard, nephew of Marvin Howard (1897–1969), who led Ocracoke's mounted Boy Scout troop in the late 1950s, and grandson of the legendary horseman Homer Howard, allowed me to use excerpts from his Web site detailing his family history with the wild ponies.

Allison Turner, biological science technician at Assateague Island National Seashore, supplied excellent information about the Maryland herd and shared Park Service photographs that vividly show the bites and kicks that occur when people get too close to wild horses.

DeAnna Locke, administrator of the Ocracoke Preservation Society, let me pore over and digitize the organization's fascinating scrapbooks, which included many pictures of the island's mounted Boy Scout troop.

Tim Ferry and Flickr user rich701 allowed me to reprint some of their unique historical photographs of the Chincoteague herd.

Craig Downer, a wild-horse ecologist and activist on the board of directors of the Cloud Foundation, shared several of his writings with me on the subject of mustang management.

Jean Bonde of the Buy-Back Babes has a contagious enthusiasm for the Chincoteague Ponies and many tales to tell. These ponies have a large cult following, and her e-mail group recounted the details of their lives—celebrating the romance of Copper Moose and Scotty's ET, pondering Rip Tide's status within Surfer Dude's band, and speculating on why Queenie and Suzy Sweetheart were wandering around the wildlife loop.

Tabetha Fenton of Barefoot Minis helped with proofreading and offered enthusiastic support.

Special thanks to my mother, Joyce Urquhart, who is an exceptionally good proofreader. She read every word of the manuscript and discovered errors that other readers missed.

My husband, Alex, is committed to giving me space in which to create and assisting me wherever possible in my creative pursuits. Besides proof-reading my manuscripts, he is the behind-the-scenes man who maintains the household, runs to the post office, and brings in the bird feeders at night so the bears don't destroy them. He is the love of my life and I am thankful every day that we are together.

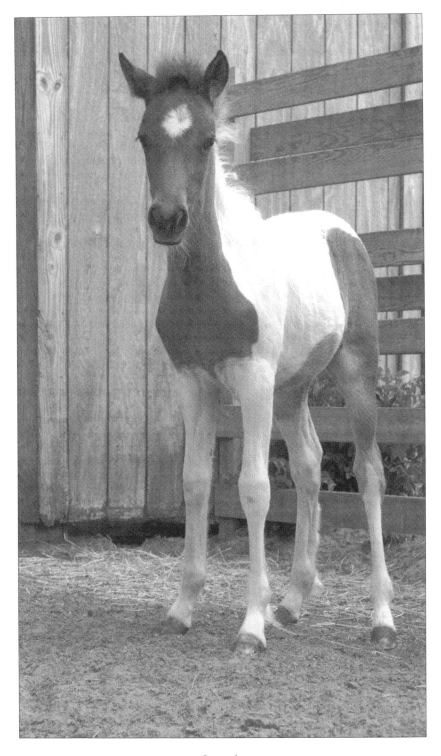

Ocracoke

About the Author

Bonnie Urquhart Gruenberg is a multifaceted person who wishes that sleep were optional. She is the author of the award-winning textbook *Birth Emergency Skills Training* (Birth Guru/Birth Muse, 2008); *Essentials of Prehospital Maternity Care* (Prentice Hall, 2005); and *Hoofprints in the Sand: Wild Horses of the Atlantic Coast* (as Bonnie S. Urquhart; Eclipse, 2002), as well as articles in publications as dissimilar as *Equus* and the *American Journal of Nursing*. She is an artist and photographer and has illustrated all her own books.

By profession, she is a Certified Nurse-Midwife and Women's Health Nurse Practitioner who welcomes babies into the world at a freestanding birth center in Lancaster County, Pa. She obtained her MSN from the University of Pennsylvania after completing her BSN at Southern Vermont College, and she spent 10 years attending births in tertiary-care hospitals before returning to out-of-hospital practice. Prior to her career in obstetrics, she worked as an urban paramedic in Connecticut.

Horses have been her passion from infancy. For nearly two decades, she has spent countless hours researching and photographing the private lives of wild horses in both Western and Eastern habitats. She has been riding, training, teaching, and learning since her early teens, from rehabilitating hard-luck horses to wrangling trail rides in Vermont and Connecticut. In her vanishing spare time, she explores the hills and hollows of Lancaster County astride her horses Andante and Sonata.

More information and a collection of her photographs can be found at her Web site, www.BonnieGruenberg.com Additional information about the Atlantic Coast horse herds is on the Web at www.WildHorse Islands.com

If you liked this book, you may enjoy other titles by the author:

The Wild Horse Dilemma: Conflicts and Controversies of the Atlantic Coast Herds (Quagga Press, 2015)
The Hoofprints Guide Series (Quagga Press, 2015)
 Assateague
 Chincoteague
 Corolla
 Ocracoke
 Shackleford Banks
 Cumberland Island

Forthcoming

Wild Horse Vacations: Your Guide to the Atlantic Wild Horse Trail with Local Attractions and Amenities (Quagga Press, 2015)
Wild Horses! A Kids' Guide to the East Coast Herds (Quagga Press, 2015)

Visit QuaggaPress.com for details.

Made in the USA
Charleston, SC
29 June 2016